# •THE 5th LIST
# •OF SHIT
# •THAT MADE
# •ME A
# •FEMINIST

Farida D.

Farida D. is an Arab gender researcher and poet, studying Arab women's everyday oppressions for over a decade. Through the process- she broke up with her hijab, set her high heels on fire, and authored a series of books. Farida's words have been on BBC Radio London, are continuously amplified by celebrities, and strolling all over social media. Contact her via email farida-d@outlook.com, or on Instagram @farida.d.author

*I can only meet you as far as I have met myself.*
*You can only meet me as far as you have met yourself.*

*How far shall we meet?*

801.

Who came
first,
the egg
or the sperm?

Who *came*
first?

802.

When we liberate women
we liberate men too.

We are made from egg
and sperm, and love too.

803.

The world of the womb
is a world of equal rights.

It doesn't care whether
you're male or female
or Black or White.

It holds you, safely.
It loves you, unconditionally.
It nourishes your limbs
until you feel alright.

The world of the womb
held us all warmly
in a swaddle.

Why can't our world
follow that model?

804.

Time is a woman.
Can't you see how the calendar of the moon
is synched with the cycle of the womb?

Life is a woman.
Can't you see that each living
being
was once inside a woman?

Earth is a woman.
Can't you see how much she suffers
under the ruling of men?


So when they say "it's a man's world"
ask them:
if "it's a man's world"
why aren't men
taking good care of it?!


\*\*\*


Our world is created by women
but it is ruled by men.

The economy
is raised
by the softness of the feminine,
but runs
on the harshness of the masculine.

This is a summary
of everything
wrong in the world.

805.

The world is running
on a masculine blueprint.

Where is the feminine?

Look at how governments are run;
making up laws and religions
on wages, on marriages, on abortions
for the best interest
of the masculine gender.

Daring to tell us it's all God's words or the nature of life
to which we must naturally surrender!

Look at how businesses are run;
cold, hard, harsh
we're taught that leaders cannot be tender.

Look at how medicine and science
focuses on males and their bodies as the norm,
there is so much that remains unknown
about the female form.
We erroneously refer to 'vulvas'
as 'vaginas',
because the only value
of a female body
is to make for the penis
a home.

Look at how schools teach us history
from a male point of view,

where is the history
that made women too?

Women aren't a new invention
or a produce of a feminist century-
women have existed
since the beginning of time,
so why fuck are we a novelty?

So much about us remains a mystery
because the patriarchy is determined
to keep us in misery.

They turned our goodness into evilness
and our strengths into weaknesses,
we're only loved when we're princesses
waiting for a prince
to give us a kiss
to wake us up
from a peaceful dream into a horrid patriarchy,
that's our reality;
we're taught that women who have a voice are seductresses and
bitches
and temptresses and witches,
that's how they justify
setting our grandmothers into flames
that's how they convince you
your sexuality, your body, your voice is to blame
that's how they break your bones
and rebuild them with shame.
Trace the history from you
all the way back to Eve,
what does the world

want you to believe
about women and what they can and cannot
do and achieve?

Silence. . .
is the only inheritance
that women are allowed to leave,
behind.

Silence. . .
is seen as kindness.

And when kindness is associated with femininity
and femininity is associated with misogyny,
this world will never want to be kind!

But without the feminine,
how can we call ourselves human*kind*?

Look around you today!
What the fuck is happening to our world?!

Why is softness, nurturing, caring,
and loving others,
seen as weakness and absurd?

Our world is running
on a masculine blueprint.

Our world is suffering
and perhaps. . .
that's the hint.

N.B. Balance your masculine and feminine energies.

806.

Backseat blow jobs
vodka shots
cigars burning
the way my body
is yearning
to numb the numbness
of an ordinary life.

Can we be happy
without money?
I'll write poetry
to your photography
we'll be starving artists
hungry
for life.

I have life in me-
I want to spend my life
without life spending me.

I want to spend the dreams saved in my piggy bank
instead of watching my swear jar collect money.

Fuck settling down
 just because you call me 'honey'.

I want to live a life that is rare and raw.
My meat is not numb enough for you to gnaw.

807.

When we had nothing
we had
each other.

But when we got money
we got fancy cars
that drove us so fast and far
away
from one another.
And we got Cuban cigars
to have something to kiss
instead of the lips
of one another.

Do you remember?

Do you remember when we used to say
that money would solve our problems one day?
We sat hand in hand
drew plans in the sand
and cried when the oceans
washed them away?
Little did we understand
the oceans knew
more than me and you,
they were saving us
from drowning
because
when we had nothing
we had nothing
to tear us away

from one another,
which is to say
that when we had nothing
we actually had
each other.

Oh what a funny thing!

When we had nothing
we actually had
everything!

808.

Society's checklist;
*Study
*Get a job
*Get married
*Buy a house
*Have kids
is inherently
capitalist.

You become labour, produce labour,
consume throughout,
and it's all based on
a gender role hierarchy.
That's why men are shamed
for not getting a job,
while women are shamed
for not getting married;
capitalism works
alongside patriarchy.

Fuck society's checklist.
Do what makes you happy.

You were not born out of a womb
that was willing to stretch and accommodate
to your own growth,
for you to force yourself
inside a box that society put forth.

809.

Richard Gere
comes up on the TV screen
that costs thousands of dollars to buy
in a Hollywood movie that costs millions of dollars to make,
inside the tent
of the local coffee shop
where I spent
hefty cents
for imported English tea and a Swiss chocolate bar.
Gere is on mute
but Umm Kulthum blasts
from a speaker of the past
yet she doesn't feel so far.
This is where we are;
in the middle of consumerism
there is colonialism
and capitalism
and poverty,
and traditionalism
and globalism
and 21st century.
In the East, yet in the West.
In the present, yet in the past.
How did we come this far?
All we know is that
here we are.

810.

In a capitalist economy,
we measure our value with money.

We attach price tags around our necks
and choke to get our cheques.

Even the way we define
how we *spend* our time
is based on productivity
and success.
We feel guilty
when we *waste* our time
on rest.

*Rest is a luxury we can't afford.*

Days off and vacations
are for the rich to hoard.

Tell me this:
in a capitalist economy
can you *save* happiness,
without having to first *spend* time
on work and stress?

811.

We are a society that values
only what we can attach a price tag to.
That is why we excel at
hard work, rewards, accumulating stuff...
And it is also why we struggle with
kindness, happiness, and love.


***


We're animals.

All we need is
something to eat
somewhere to sleep
to have sex and to shit.

The whole American Dream?
That's really it.

812.

If you want to know
how slow time moves
visit the poorest villages
in the poorest countries
and observe how
they make it through the night.

You will never know
how slow time moves
in a money-hungry, hurry economy
where the idiot behind you, honks at you
to pass the red light.

***

Time is a social construction
invented by the clock of capitalism.

They tell you to sleep at night
so that they crack you in the light
and steal your day.

And over time
as you age
they discard you away.

Artists don't sleep at night.
Dreamers don't sleep at night-
that's when they play.

Time is an infinite resource
that capitalist clocks captured
and structured
into a finite resource
with a price tag and a deadline
and night and day.


For your time on earth
what are you willing to pay?

813.

We think
we're the consumers.

But what we don't realize
is that we're being consumed.


A 9-5 job
steals your most productive hours;
that's why you're too tired
to do anything else after work
except for lying down
in front of the TV
consuming ads and media
that convince you to buy
the means to being free,
and then you go to sleep
to wake up again
to go to that dead-end job
to pay bills
that keep you in captivity.

I don't want to spend my life
writing cheques for regret.

I want to spend life, not money.

No one gets buried with their wealth.
All that we take is whatever is leftover
from our lack of health.

Live your dream.

It's not a cliché.

Don't let that dream continue to sleep
after you wake up each day.


***


Do you know why
the uncertainty
of the hustle
feels more fulfilling
than the security
of a job that's 9-5?

It's because our ancestors
were hunter-gatherers;
the bustle
of the hustle
kept them alive.

814.

When people look at a tall
glorious skyscraper
they see glory.
But as for me, I feel sorry.
For all the lives that silently
tumbled down
during the construction.
We read them as random statistics
while they are family destruction.
How many people lost
their father, brother, lover?
Who risked their lives
just to build this fancy tower?
For rich families to live
in the sky,
poor families have to give
their men up
and let them
die.


N.B. Falls are the leading cause of death in construction. These deaths
are preventable. (Source: OSHA, Occupational Safety and Health
Administration - United States Department of Labor).

815.

The problem with capitalism
is that it tells the working class
they're poor because they buy
overpriced Starbucks coffee,
instead of telling Starbucks
to reasonably price their coffee
or, you know, to pay their working class employees
a decent salary.

That is how the rich get richer, for sure;
they take from, and never pay back,
the poor.

And then they market their products as part of the "good life"
to keep the poor spending more.


The poor are kept poor
by being paid minimum wage
by the rich
(and that's also how
the rich stay rich).


\*\*\*



Who is the thief?

The one who steals?
Or the one who makes up the rules

25

to work in their favour
about what constitutes stealing?


Who is the thief?

The poor who can't pay the rich,
for the means to eat?
Or the rich who doesn't pay the poor,
just to sustain a position among the elite?


You cannot get rich
without exploiting the poor.

816.

You know who suffers
the most
when you ban
abortions?

Working class people-
because they are the ones
who won't be able to afford
to travel elsewhere for abortions.


You know who suffers
the most
when you deny
universal healthcare?

Working class people-
because they are the ones
who won't be able to afford
paying medical bills.


You know who suffers
the most
when you don't have
universal access to education?

Working class people-
because they are the ones
who won't be able to afford
to pay for education

that pays them with a better paid job.
How else can the cycle of poverty
stop?


You know who suffers
the most
when you don't vote?

Working class people-
because they are the ones
disadvantaged
by the same policies
that give the rich privilege.


I urge you to see
that first and foremost
the ones who suffer the most
are the poor that are kept poor
by the systemic oppressions of society.

***


Making healthcare a luxury
is like making oxygen a luxury;
breathing shouldn't be a luxury.

Food shouldn't be a luxury.
Education shouldn't be a luxury.
Transportation shouldn't be a luxury.

Shelter shouldn't be a luxury.
Safety shouldn't be a luxury.


Healthcare, food, education, transportation, shelter, and safety
are only made a luxury
because there are people who use them as a means
to sustain their wealth.


We all deserve to live without worrying
about preventable death.



N.B. Staying alive shouldn't be a privilege.

817.

"The death penalty is a blessing"
he said,
"I'd rather die than spend my whole life in a prison bed".

So I said; "Listen
prison
and the
death penalty
should both be abolished".

He looked at me astonished.

Prison and the death penalty
are designed by the rich
to have a way to legally lock up and kill
the poor who step out of line.

Who wrote the books of law
and the books of the divine?

Who put the rules?
Who decides how they are broken?

Our world is broken.

The rich steal from the poor
and run free.
If the poor steal back
they are locked in captivity.

"But what about murderers?" he asks

"don't they deserve the death penalty?"

"Who gives the law a right
to murder?
When you murder a murderer
you're a murderer too!
I don't care if the law has permitted you!
No one should have a permit
to kill another person!"

So he says "then what's the solution?!"

The solution is
abolishing poverty.
Everyone has a right to access
food and necessity.
We need to abolish
the circumstances
that lead people
to a life of crime.

And as for murderers
tell me
has the persistence of the death penalty
abolished murder in our day and time?

Perhaps we can try another strategy-
fund sectors that educate people,
instead of giving the law
the role of the devil and the divine.

N.B. Amnesty International holds that the death penalty breaches human rights. For 40 years, Amnesty has been campaigning to abolish the death penalty around the world.

818.

"The Coronavirus pandemic
has created equality",
they say,
"whether you're rich or poor,
you can get infected any day".

That's bullshit.

Coronavirus disregards the poor,
they are more prone to the pandemic
for sure.

Let me tell you why,
you need to follow certain rules
to reduce your risk of infection
and the chance you may die.

You need to stay at home,
but what about those without a home?
You need to have clean water and soap,
but what about those without clean water and soap?
You need to use your ATM card
no cash, no pennies,
but what about the homeless who have no bank account let alone any
money?
They tell you to stay at home
and order your grocery online,
but guess who is going to process your order and fulfil the delivery on
time?
People!
People who get paid minimum wage

forced to put their lives on the frontline
because they need that wage to live
(to barely live).

The Coronavirus hasn't created equality;
if anything it is begging us to see
our horrific classism reality.


N.B. The less affluent face more risks during the Coronavirus
pandemic. (Source: brookings.edu).

819.

"Money can't buy happiness"
is a capitalist mantra
written all over mugs and magnets
sold in multimillion dollar stores,
to keep the poor
locked into a mentality
that keeps the wealthy secure.

Money may not buy happiness-
but it can pay the bills for sure.


                              ***




Money is power.

And when you buy stuff,
and as you give your money to corporations,
you also give them power.

Each dollar spent on what you bought
each dollar you spend, is bought
as a vote,
that you give
for corporations
to survive.

Which corporations

do you want to shape our world?
Which corporate values
do you want to thrive?

820.

Art is labour.
Activism is labour.

And if you constantly
expect me
to give you my art and activism
for free;
how are you any better
than the capitalist economy
that constantly takes
advantage of you and me?

Yes, the ultimate goal
of my art and activism
is for you;
to empower you
to help you
stand tall
on your feet.

But for me to do that full-time,
I also need to
be able to eat.

\*\*\*

Art, from painting to writing, is awareness.

Perhaps artists

aren't paid nearly enough,
because the capitalist system wants to discourage them
from pursuing a lifetime making people aware
of the injustices and oppressions of the system.


N.B. Normalize compensating independent artists. So that more of us
can afford to depend on our art.

821.

Labour exploitation
sometimes looks like
requiring us to take a loan to study
which then allows us to get a job
to work
to repay that loan.


It is a vicious cycle of capitalism.

They lend us money
to ensure we spend
a lifetime
chained behind a desk.

822.

"Low-skilled labour"
is a term invented by capitalism
to justify "low wages".

Labour, by nature, is intensive
and "low-skilled labour" is particularly intensive
because the rich get richer
only when exploiting the poor.


N.B. There is no such thing as "low-skilled" labour; only "low-valued" labour.

823.

What the fuck do you mean by
"are you a *working* mother?!"

All mothers
are working mothers!

\*\*\*

Are you upset that due to COVID-19
you're working from home
with a cut to your usual pay?
Wives and mothers have always worked at home
with absolutely no pay.

N.B. Women make up 39% of global employment but account for
54% of overall job losses during the Coronavirus pandemic, as the
virus significantly increased the burden of unpaid care carried out in
the homes by women. (Source: McKinsey Global Institute).

824.

Those rich men
became rich
because they *underpaid*
the labour running their business,
and *never paid*
the women raising their children.

\*\*\*

You are half sperm; half egg.
But you are not equally bred.

A man created you from
9 minutes of pleasure;
a woman created you from
9 months of unpaid labour.

N.B. Facts.

825.

Have you noticed
how the patriarchy
capitalizes on our bodies,
as soon as we get pregnant?

As if the sperm enters our bodies
as an investment,
with the return being
patriarchal ownership
of the stocks in our ovaries
and the factories
of our reproductive facilities;
our agency is fired
for being too costly.

It's as if we are no longer humans when,
we are being used
to produce humans.

826.

Women run the world, quietly.
Our backbones
build homes.
We raise generation upon generation
without being paid.
We get treated as if it is in our nature
to be maids.
Men get praised
loudly,
for the same work that women
do quietly.
Men run the world,
creating power
out of money and social class.
But without the labour of love
that women freely give,
this world economy would collapse.

\*\*\*

If we ask you to repay
the amount of women's unpaid labour,
the economy
would be
in debt forever.

827.

If we had a penny for each time
a man told a woman to smile;
we'll be able to close the unequal pay gap in a day,
and no man will ever ask us to smile again
because we'll always be smiling anyway!

828.

Isn't it interesting
how women's labour at home is unpaid
and women are expected to offer it for free-
yet when the same labour is performed
by a capitalist economy
we are charged enormous sums for it?

Next time you pay for
food at a restaurant
fancy coffee,
childcare services
or even laundry-
I want you to remember
all the women
who do all this shit, all day
in every home, for free.
Our backbones the blueprint
our sweat the fuel,
for the capitalist economy.
And how we're not only conditioned
to accept not being paid for our labour,
but how our free labour is normalized
as our moral duty
by the patriarchy.

***

You know why most chefs are men?
Because unlike women,
men won't cook at home for free.

They value their labour.

Unpaid labour is not
on their speciality.


N.B. Only 17% of chef positions in the UK are held by women.
(Source: Office for National Statistics).

829.

The size of her room
is the size
of an average grave
under a tomb.
She leaves it just to cook and clean
and babysit kids
who will never ever know
the life her own kids
had to forgo,
for their mother
to work in another
modern country
as a modern-day slave.
She works around the clock
with no breaks,
a human trapped in a hamster wheel
with no brakes.
She cooks for everyone,
but only eats leftovers.
She sleeps after everyone,
but only on her own shoulders.
She gets beaten and raped
as part of the job,
(no one told her that's
part of the contract
when she signed up).
She isn't allowed to leave the house
(except if she has to run more errands and chores).
She isn't allowed a phone to call her spouse
(because she might call strange men and whores).
She often doesn't get her full pay,

and gets told that if she doesn't accept that
she can no longer stay.
And she doesn't accept it but she still doesn't leave,
because she can't afford to lose
whatever little pennies she'll receive.
Her lifestyle is normalized
to the extent that no one sees anything wrong.
Her only choice becomes
to be strong.
But I am begging you, not to play along
with a system
designed to abuse
and use
Asian women
who leave their homes to work at your home
for a better life,
but end up in a strife
that cannot be reasonably foreseen.

What price are Asian domestic workers paying,
to keep your kids fed
and your fucking house clean?!


***


Is it really that hard?

To throw out your own garbage
and pick up your own shit?

Is it really that much of a fuss?

So much so
that we uphold a Kafala system
with slavery conditions
because we need to hire
Asian domestic workers
at minimum wage
who leave their homes
and their families
and cross oceans
to come live with us,
just to pick up
our own shit for us?!


N.B. Abolish the Kafala system.

830.

Women have been used like houses.

Wombs house men-
rent-free
not allowed eviction
via abortion.

Vaginas house men-
they tear into a hymen
they imagine
to bleed
to come
alive
for them.

Chests house men-
they nurse on comfort
they can always depend on
for support
as solid as concrete,
as they ignore
the sounds
of the hearts beneath
that beat.

We are human.

Women are not houses
with gardens mowed
pristine and neat,
for you to retreat.

Women are not houses
with 'welcome' mats
for your dirty feet.

Women are not houses
that you leave to go to hotels
whenever you want to cheat.

Women are not houses.

We are human.

We wear and tear.
We hurt and pain.

Humans are not built
to be houses that shelter others
from the rain.


We all hurt the same.

831.

In a capitalist society
a woman is the capital
her body is the commodity
exchanged from ex-boyfriend to current boyfriend
from father to husband
and if she objects
to being an object
or if she dared
to reclaim her pleasure-
men would send
the God they made-believe to pretend
to punish her
for sinning,
because how can else can they continue to control her
if she's winning?

832.

When women are viewed as commodities
it is not so surprising
that men objectify, dehumanize, and ignore our rights.

You won't think to think about the rights
of a fleshlight.

***

When you sexualize women
you see them as objects for gratification
and when you see them as objects for gratification
you stop seeing them as human
and when you stop seeing them as human
you stop treating them as human
and you stop treating them as human
you oppress them.

833.

"SEX SELLS"
they say.

But when it's only
the female sex
that is used as a marketing ploy to sell-
it's not *sex* that sells
it's *sexism* that sells.

***

Women's bodies have been used
to sell everything
from fast food to cars.

Women's bodies have been claimed
as prizes of victory
at the end of wars.

Women's bodies have been reduced
to being wives
and mothers-
to make men
and to make them
into fathers.

But what baffles me the most
is when a woman decides
to own, enjoy, or profit from
the body she's in-

men are quick to tell her
that *God says*
she's committing a sin.

834.

When a woman uses
her own body
for her own profit
for her own benefit
for her own pleasure,
she is shamed.

Why?

Because only a man
is allowed to use
a woman's own body
for his own profit
for his own benefit
for his own pleasure.

The patriarchy
and capitalism
shame women
for profiting
off their own body-
because they
want women to give
their bodies away
for free;
as sexual lovers
and as incubators
turned into mothers.

Patriarchy and capitalism
work for one another,

at the expense of women
who are expected
to accept not being compensated
for how much they suffer.

835.

Women will never have equality
when there is no equality
in the bedroom and the kitchen;
when we do all the cooking and cleaning
and get none of the orgasms.

For equality
women need to reclaim the free labour
they pay for with their bodies.

It starts in your house.
It starts with your spouse.
It starts with your body.

Set the laws that set you free.

Live your life by the rules
that you write
the way you want them to be.

836.

I left a life of money
to be
independent
financially.

I married a man, who unlike my father, isn't wealthy.
We both depend monthly
on a salary.

He spends more than me.
I save more than him.

Perhaps this isn't a coincidental whim.

Perhaps he is afraid of being rich
and I am afraid of being poor.

Perhaps this is how we uphold
the class system we both deeply
abhor.

837.

Everyone was against my marriage.

My choice of husband not only came from
a different religious sect,
but also financially
he was considered inept.
He owns just the shirt on his back
and the struggles his own father had to endure.
They told me, he won't afford to maintain the life of luxury
my father has coated me in, for sure.

But all I could hear from their concerns-
is that as a woman my lifestyle depends
on what the man who owns me earns.

So I studied
obtained the highest degree,
got a job
to secure myself financially.

And I vowed to marry the man I love
for I have a far grander plan;
not on a father, nor on a husband
I won't ever depend on a man.

838.

As a girl, they told me
that when I grow up
unlike my grandmother before me;
I have a "choice".

Gone are the days where women are
puppets that scream NO
while no
one hears their voice.

But as soon as I wasn't a girl anymore
they arranged my marriage to a rich man I've never met before.
They took my choice and my voice
and wrote my freewill as an invoice.


In a second, my world shattered.


I told them I love another man
in the fairytales the princess picks her prince,
but to them, none of that mattered.

For I wasn't picking a prince
the man I love didn't own a castle-
they told me, love cannot survive
in a life that is financially a hassle.

I was just 19.

They wanted me to marry a man

I have never even seen.

The only difference between,
my life and the life of my grandmother
is that I was living in another
time.
The rules didn't change;
she didn't pick her husband
and they won't let me pick mine.

And they still dare to say
"women have a choice".

They already picked my wedding date
sealed like a business deal, my entire fate
told me I was too young to debate.
Yet, the irony
is that they didn't think I was too young to marry!
Selling me in a hurry
to a man hungry
for popping cherry.

And despite all that
they wouldn't hesitate
to keep saying "women have a choice"-
to sound progressive
as they insidiously bait
while their guilty conscience can rejoice.

In the end I had choice
that much is true.
But let me tell you
what I had to do,

for that "choice" to be given to me.
I had to lock myself in my room
for an eternity
and I refused to eat
as they watched me suffer
with a blind eye.
Even my own mother
who knows how hard it is
to give up a lover, for another
strange man to fuck the world
between her thigh,
wouldn't soften
when she heard how hard I'd cry.
She cut all forms of communication from the man whom I already told her
that without his love, I would die.


For that "choice" my blood
turned into the tears.
For that "choice" I had to fight
for ten years.


This is the first time I speak this part of my story.
For what was done to me, I will never be
sorry.

And when they say, to this day, to my dismay
that "women have a choice"-
I quickly finish their sentence by adding
"but not without a hefty invoice!"

839.


"You can be anything"
reads the slogan of *Barbie*
perched on the pink shelf in the kid's toy store,
and the *Barbie* options sold in our local shop
are only four:
a mermaid, a baker, a ballerina, and a fairy princess.
What kind of fuckery
is this?


When you tell a little girl
"you can be anything"
then present her with limited options,
what is she supposed to think
about what it means to be 'anything'?


What it's saying
is,
"you can be anything"
as long as your choice
is to become
one
of the options approved by patriarchy.


That is not freedom!
When you tell little girls
that they can be,
anything,
you carry the responsibility

to not distort their understanding
on what it means to be
anything.
You carry the responsibility
to act accordingly
you don't just make statements full of promises and possibility
and then deliver
a script of patriarchy.


I don't want to teach my daughter
bullshit in the name of feminism
packaged in pink capitalism-
real freedom to be
means there are
no limits
no pre-determined options
no script to follow.


Marketers think,
feminism is something
they can package and sell.
They think let's just make money
out of ideas that do well.


But it doesn't work that way-
performative activism
reeks of desperation
just to increase sales each day.

Don't get me wrong,
the concept is strong:
teach your daughters that they can be,
anything they want to be.
But they don't need permission
or to choose from limited options
when deciding what to be.


The sky is their limit.
Fuck patriarchy, fuck capitalism,
and fuck *Barbie*.


N.B. Fuck performative feminism.

840.


Like boneless chicken wings
society broke me
battered me
hammered me
dressed me
in hot
BBQ sauce.

But I am not a piece of meat
on the menu,
or a side dish that you toss.

Fuck your capitalist beauty ideals,
where companies and men
invent my insecurities
to feed off me
from my already, unequal salary
leaving me at loss.

Take me off that menu,
I am not here to fulfil you
or to fill you-
I am not the food, or the menu,
I am the boss.

841.

*Cinderella*
reinforces the idea that
makeup and a fancy dress
(i.e. beauty ideals and capitalism)
are what makes one desirable,
and without them
you are barely recognizable.

The prince, a wealthy capitalist,
relied on a pair of glass slippers
to find *Cinderella* because he could not recognize her
outside of the "capitalist idea of beauty".

This leads one to ponder that perhaps
the prince never fell in love with *Cinderella* herself
as the story has been told-
perhaps what he fell in love with
is merely a reflection of the world he upholds?

N.B. Deconstruct your favourite childhood fairytales. For they carry
so much of what you carry around as normalized ideas.

842.

The patriarchy teaches women
that our most valuable asset
is our body;
guard it from all men
but not your husband
(as if husbands don't rape),
don't be too fat or too thin
(just keep it in the "right" shape).
Shave your legs
but don't dress
like you want sex.
And if you have sex
do it for free
for if you charge money
you're a whore.

All those mixed messages
and more...

And yet when we reclaim our bodies
and decide who to fuck
whether we shave or not
or what to wear,
we are shamed
like how could we even dare,
to control our most valuable asset
instead of groom it as a commodity
that men can trade and share.

The patriarchy teaches women
that our bodies

are our most valuable assets,
and yet,
when we reclaim our bodies
it's as if we are thieves
stealing from the patriarchy.

843.


Today
I looked at my old photos
from years ago,
from a time when I thought I was fat.

*Look at that...*
I thought,
*I wasn't actually fat.*
*Or I wasn't as fat as I am now.*

Years later
I know I will look at my old photos
from today
from a time when I thought I was fat.

*Look at that...*
I would think,
*I wasn't actually fat.*
*Or I wasn't as fat as I am now.*

Am I the only one who does that?
Or do all women sow
seeds of shame?

And I keep looking at my older photos
the same;
at that time
when I didn't think I was fit enough
or pretty enough
I clearly remember all the lack of love
I gave myself,

digesting the hate
that comes as the price
of the beauty standards
that never let you appreciate
yourself;
always waiting to be
always wishing to be
somebody (some *body*) else.

And I look at myself now
scold myself for being a fat cow
and then scold myself for giving a damn.
And I know that years later
I will wonder why I didn't love myself
just the way I am?

And I look at myself now
again and again
squinting to unsee the shame
and I wonder
to my utter, utter
dismay-
do women always wait for tomorrow
to love themselves
just the way they are
today?

N.B. According to Mayo Clinic, body dysmorphic disorder is a
mental health disorder in which one cannot stop thinking about
perceived flaws in appearance.

844.

I must have thick hair,
but a thin body.

And to achieve this ideal
of thick and thin,
I'm constantly trapped between
adding hair extensions to my head
and ripping the fat off my skin.

845.

And even if you lose
so much weight
until you're only skin and bone,
until you're only the shadow
of a ghost.
And you ask society
the question that haunts you the most;
"am I good enough now?"
They'll say;
"you've overdone it- go eat some toast".

You will never be good enough
for a standard designed
to never see you as good enough.

***

Body shaming
in the name of health
is like
terrorism
in the name of religion.

846.

She was in her 30's
when she became a widow.
That was almost
10 years ago.

In her 40's now
she's ready to date again.
But the dating market
is not the same.

The younger men want young women.
The older men want even younger women.

Young is beauty.

And she...

She was mourning her beauty.

And right into her vulnerability
marched the cosmetic industry.
They convinced her to fix herself
as if she's the problem
not the way society views everyone else
who isn't a perky
twenty
year old.

Forty isn't even fucking old.

What lies are we buying

that capitalism sold?

Veneer teeth.
Botox cheeks.
New breasts.
A little nip and tuck
for the rest.

Now she felt
she looked her best.

Now men started to look her way.
But they couldn't see
the price she had to pay,
what she had to do
for men to love her again.

Her body was in constant pain.


How much are women willing to pay
(and not just financially),
to be loved
by men
who have distorted definitions
of beauty?

847.

She died
because she won't let
the gender labels and beauty standard myths
die.

Breast cancer, unlike gender
and beauty standards,
isn't a lie.

She refused to remove her breasts
because she worried without them
she won't be seen as womanly again.

So the cancer from her breasts
began to eat her brain.

She died.

She died with her breasts intact.

She died and I wish I can bring her back,
to tell her
that her life matters
more than beauty standards,
that she is a woman
because she identifies as one,
that gender labels
are just for games and fun.

She died and I can't tell her now,
but I can tell everyone;

Having breasts,
does not make you a woman.
Having a vagina,
does not make you a woman.
Having periods,
does not make you a woman.
Having curves,
does not make you a woman.
Identifying as a woman,
is the only thing
that makes you a woman.

And in the same vein;

Having balls,
does not make you a man.
Having a penis,
does not make you a man.
Having sperm,
does not make you a man.
Having muscles,
does not make you a man.
Identifying as a man,
is the only thing
that makes you a man.

Gender labels and beauty standards
are a social myth and lie-
if you want to participate in them, do it for fun,
but don't let them be the reason
you die.

N.B. In memory of a late relative of mine- who preferred to die than to get a mastectomy.

848.

My friend got a boob job
because she felt
she was the only woman with breasts
that were hanging down low.

But when I showed her how far
mine would go,
she wondered what was normal
and what she was supposed to feel.

Why doesn't the media ever show us
breasts that are real?


                              ***


Saggy breasts
aren't ugly-
they're normal.

Stretch marks
aren't ugly-
they're normal.

Flabby guts
aren't ugly-
they're normal.

Cellulite thighs
aren't ugly-

they're normal.

Normal
isn't ugly-
it's normal.

Beauty standards
aren't normal.

849.

I'm late for work again
because I slept in
just like the men,
but getting ready for work
for men and women isn't the same.
Men can sleep in and still be on time,
but when I sleep in, I run out of time.

How?

Women and men
don't have the same clocks.
Men save more of their time
because they aren't expected
to give any fucks.

Men need 10 minutes
to brush their teeth, pee,
take a shower with a 3 in 1 shampoo, conditioner, and body gel,
you'd say they're looking swell
without knowing that they wipe their face with the same towel,
that they wipe their ass with
(trust me, that's not a myth).
Then they put on the same shirt and pants they wore 10 years ago,
pop out the door, all ready to go.

But women are assigned the script
to play the longer unedited version
of the same show.

We need hours

from the night before
to plan our outfit, because we can't wear the same thing every day.
After all, we just exist as objects in the workplace
to make it look pretty,
(that's why we get unequal pay).

In the morning we have to do what men do
brush our teeth, pee, shower too
but here's where it gets complicated;
we don't have washing products
that are 3 in 1
(or forest animals to help, or a magic fairy wand)
we have to actually spend time on hair and makeup and beyond
looking no less glam
than Beyoncé in her latest song.
This shit takes time
and that time is shit long.
In order not to have chipped nail polish,
I have chipped sleep,
extra hours of my life spent
that men get to keep.

I'm late for work again
because I slept in
just like the men
and then just like the women
I took time to get ready.

I'm late, but I'm playing the roles of men and women
so instead of a warning from my boss
I expect fucking confetti!

N.B. According to the National Sleep Foundation's 2007 *Sleep in America* poll, women have no time for sleep and stay-at-home mothers are more likely to sleep poorly. Women's lack of sleep affects almost all aspects of their lives- making them late for work, stressed out, too tired for sex, and left with little time to socialize.

850.

Beauty standards
are time-specific and contextual-
and they change based on
what men find
sexual.

851.

Diet culture and beauty standards tell us
to constantly be thinner, leaner, finer, paler...
that that's the way to be more beautiful,
but based on whose beauty ideals?

Being told that being thin and fair is beautiful
and that being beautiful is to be thin and fair
is a White beauty concept
that leaves Black and Brown women in despair,
always striving for an ideal
they can never achieve
and use their failure to believe,
they were never ever
meant to be...
an ideal standard for beauty.

\*\*\*

Beauty standards reflect
sexism (set as an expectation for women),
racism (defined as mostly White and light),
capitalism (can be bought through cosmetics/surgery, and is
considered a woman's social capital to trade),
sizeism (reserved for smaller sizes),
ableism (reserved for certain bodies),
ageism (reserved for youth).

Beauty standards are inherently patriarchal.

It is not a coincidence that the epitome of beauty, *the girl next door*, is a White young thin woman. While any other beauty, say a Black young curvy woman, is at best exotic or at worst a fetish.

852.

"I gotta tell you, I have a fetish for Asian women" he told me, as he
gently undressed me,
"your almond eyes, your silky hair-
I wanna roll my tongue all over you
like a Buddhist prayer".


"What about me?" I pulled back,
"What about my personality?
My voice?
What about my choice
to be or not be a fetish?
Do I get a say in any of this
fantasy?!
Look at me!
Don't fucking disrespect me,
I am bone and heart and skin.
I am ancestry. I am history.
I am religion.
I don't exist
to be your fucking fetish-
I am a person!"


N.B. Every year millions of young people in China undergo an
operation called "double eyelid surgery" where the skin around the
eye is reshaped. (Source: South China Morning Post).

853.

*Exotic?*

I look at the constellations
that make up my face,
my plump lips
my almond eyes
my Brown pigments
that I was taught
by every Hollywood movie
by every Western channel on TV
to see
as *exotic.*

I am, to myself, an 'other'.

Even when my bones
are the only ones I've known,
taken after my own
mother.

I am, to myself, an 'other'.

In a world that sees the likes of me
as exotic, Oriental,
just a fetish
that men may fantasize about
to get their sperm lined up
erect, like the soldiers
who stole my land
ready to exit their balls.

I am a moment of pleasure
dressed in the souls,
of a thousand ancestors
before me.

I am history,
of oppression
built into the DNA of my skin.

Re-born with every gaze
that sees my face,
as exotic.

*Exotic?*

Is that all that the world can see?

I can't believe that they made me believe
that's all I can ever be.

I can hear the weeps
of my ancestry.

854.

Growing up
there was no *Disney* princess
that looked like me.
*Pocahontas* was my favourite
because she was the closest
to what I see
when I look in the mirror
in my brown skin
on my black hair
full lips
and curved hips.

Representation matters
because it told me, as a child, that I matter
simply because I exist.

855.

I grew up in a White man's world.

He is the God, not seen but heard.
He is the herald
of my Brown life.
I eat the food he makes
wear the clothes he designed
watch the TV shows he produced
until they replay in my mind
until I memorize the script
of how to be
everything that wasn't me.
Until I play my Brown skin
into a role that is as White as I can be.

Until White becomes my mentality.
Until White becomes my reality.
Until White colonizes, my Brown body.

When I was in high school
the boys would drool
over Madonna and Britney Spears,
but if I dressed the same way
I'd be slut-shamed to tears.
White clothes dressing my Brown body
is like freedom undressing fears.
Because even the right to being
a woman who is a sexual being
is White.
A Brown woman has honour
planted between her thighs-

she must water it, until she dies.


As a child I did not realize,
that Santa is also White
and Snow White is White
because White became invisible to me;
it is the default, the standard,
it is not a race.
Everyone who isn't White is an "other",
my mirror told me that I was another
Brown face.
White has taught me
to be embarrassed of my ethnicity
of my backward Brown ancestry.
My Muslim traditions
are all suspicions
even the way I call for Allah
is a form of terrorism.


I grew up in a White man's world-
even my fingernails are colonized;
I replace henna with nail polish
and watch my grandmother's tears
paint her eyes,
as she recalls the days of the past
longing for a life she couldn't pass
down to me
because it's not trendy
because it's not Gucci
because it's not White.


I grew up in a White man's world-
and I believed that White

is the freedom
without realizing it feared
my light.

856.

Let's redefine beauty
from what you *look* like
to how you *feel* like.

Let beauty be that feeling
in your soul,
not about what you look like at all.

***

Strip off those
fashionable clothes.
Erase the beauty standards
you never chose.
And like a Goddess stripping off
the fuss of the divine-
meet yourself
for the very first time.

857.

*Rapunzel!*
*Rapunzel!*
Cut off your hair-
those beauty standards will get lost
when you don't give them a trail!

858.

Dear Girl,
This world will teach you
that your body's only value
is in being pretty.
They will define pretty as a narrow grave box
and give you the shovel, to bury yourself in.
You'll choke underneath
your own skin.
This is the patriarchal prison;
profiting from the insecurity
of your body parts
at the meat-market of capitalism.

Girl, no one will tell you this
so you need to constantly remind yourself;
you are worth much more than
your weight on the scale,
you are not the male gaze
you've learned to please
even when looking in your own mirror.
The patriarchy invents beauty standards
that constantly change, so you'll constantly spend
on the next staple.

But your body is just a vessel
and pretty is just a label.

859.

During childhood,
I don't recall my mother
ever
commenting on my appearance.
But my father
always told me
that I was pretty.

In adulthood,
I never cared
what other women
thought of my looks,
but I craved men's
physical validation
of me.

Moral of the story:

Dads-
don't tell your daughter
she's pretty,
instead tell her
she's pretty
powerful.
And then she'll grow
to gravitate towards the men
who seek to see her grow,
instead of the men
who want her just for show.

Because girls and women are so

much more than
pretty.


***


"Pretty" is a label
that is packed in packages
sold with hefty price tags
to turn women
into packages
freely available
for the consumption of men.

860.

I've spent so much time
looking in the mirror
to look for
the affirmations
of society.

But I couldn't find them,
you know why?

It's because the reflection
in the mirror
isn't of society.

That reflection
in the mirror
is of me.

\*\*\*


I will not apologize to my mirror
for not being slimmer.

I will not look into my face
and apologize for taking space.

I will not look at my cellulite with sorrow.
I will not dream of how
I can look better tomorrow.

I will not smooth out
the wrinkles around my eyes,

go on a smoothie diet
or believe other diet culture lies.

That pouch in the middle of my body
carried my baby into life
and it now carries all the food I love
I will never look at a plate and restrain myself
or say I've had enough,
while stomach is still growling.
I won't punish my gut
for the way it is rolling.

I will not apologize to my mirror.
I will not apologize to myself.
I will not apologize to my man.

My mirror owes me
an apology
for not letting me be
for shaming me,
for the way I am.

861.

I don't need to *lose* weight
to *gain* your acceptance.

I carry those extra pounds in me
oh so very gladly...
it is not at all heavy
to carry the weight
of being happy.

\*\*\*

The only weight
I need to lose
is the weight of
the patriarchy
on my life.

Feminism is my cardio.

862.

The trees
have brown trunks
with marks
and stretches
and leaves that fall
and branches that roll
and bend
imperfectly.
Yet when I look
at a tree
all that I see
is life
with a beauty
that is extraordinary.

The trees
are not unlike
my body.

863.

I am a museum
of natural art and history.

Look at me.

Look at the beauty lines
that society calls stretch marks
that society convinced you
are ugly.

Look at me.

Look at the constellations of stars
twinkling in the dark of my skin
that society convinced you are flaws.
Look at the mazes around my eyes
they tell you about the laws
of life.

I have lived.

This body has lived
through happiness and sadness
and heartbreaks and tears
and solace and fears
and so many years...

I am a museum
of natural art and history.
I am not a clone

of a beauty standard-
I don't want your cosmetic surgery.

864.

It's normal to have
what society calls
'physical flaws'.
And it's normal to feel
insecure about them.

What's not normal is
your conditioning
of being shamed for them,
and thus your urgency
to constantly
apologize for them.

Your 'physical flaws'-
are a social construct
and a profit cause.
The beauty industry
survives,
from your belief in
beauty myth lies.

Unlearn. Be free.
And realize.

***

Our bodies are houses.

Soft and hard.

Cracked and scarred.

Our bodies are houses
housing memories,
like that childhood home
that you grew up in
on the prairie.

Our bodies aren't meant
to be moulded and cut
to fit into a standard
frame.

Look at the houses around
your block;
no two are exactly the same.

Yes, perhaps,
there's always greener grass
or a higher fence-
but inside your own house is where
you feel your best,
you let down your guards
and your defence.

Our bodies are houses
and in yours
you have a safe space.
Our bodies are houses
not projects for capitalism
to vandalize and deface.

Our bodies are

not for the beauty industry
to refurbish
to refurnish
to redecorate
to renovate
to paint,
or to make homely for guests
who always have a complaint.

Our bodies are houses
and they are our houses
which means
they're only for us
to acquaint.

865.

When you treat your body
like an enemy
the only beneficiary
of your insecurity
is the beauty industry
created by the patriarchy.

\*\*\*

The most radical revolution begins
when a woman loves herself, as is,
in a world that convinces
her to do otherwise-
because so many industries
profit from her insecurities
without making her realize.

Lo and behold-
loving yourself
is THE greatest love story
you were never told!

866.

Self-love
is radical
in a world
that has
normalized
self-doubt.


*** 


Don't let
the world
change you.

Instead,
change
the world
by being you.

867.

"Can I change the world?"
I asked the girl in the mirror
looking back at me.

"You are the world"
she replies, at the fully grown woman
she can now see,
"and look how much you have changed!"


***


No, you don't change the world.

You change you.

You believe in you;
in unlearning toxic bullshit
and healing you,
and then...in a blink...

The world will change, too.

868.

I feel feminine
in my short boyish hair
and my Frida furry eyebrows
with a bright lipstick
that speaks truth like a dare.

I feel feminine
in my subtle stubble
hairy legs,
my natural beauty
was born with my sex.

I feel feminine
in every way that is opposite
to what society defines as femininity-
because to me, being feminine,
is all about daring
to embrace my natural body.


***



Women don't shave their legs for men-
that is such a cliché.

We shave them for our duvet.

869.

My darling-
they tell you
that you are
too loud
too quiet
too immodest
too modest
too bitchy
too pushy
because in this world
they never want to hear
or see you, too.

*Too.*

870.

We live in a world
that hands out
*more* rewards
to women
for being *less*.

You're *more* feminine,
when your voice is *less* assertive.

You're *more* respectable,
when you show *less* skin on purpose.

You're *more* sexy
when your body takes *less* space.

You're *more* beautiful
when you have *less* of a frown on your face.

You're *more*
when you're *less*.

Nonetheless
(none-the-*less*),
I will not be *less*.
Because those rewards, given to me
aren't actually for me
they are for a world that will always see
my femininity, my modesty,
my sexiness, my beauty
as *less*.

871.

I want to destroy that broken record
that keeps playing in my head;
telling me
*I'm not good enough, smart enough, pretty enough, thin enough-*
*do this or that instead.*

I'm too tired of listening to that broken record
like a lullaby that gives me nightmares
I'm trying hard to forget.

\*\*\*

We are much more than
our bodies
our beauty
our femininity
our wombs
our fertility.

As women,
we are much more than
what the patriarchy values us for.

As women,
we are much more
we are much more.

872.

They want us to be like children.

Hairless.
Ageless.
Voiceless.
Dependant.
Helpless.
Naive.

Non-threatening
in what we are capable to achieve.

They want us to be like children
that they can legally have sex with-
that's why they don't care about our
consent or pleasure,
that's why they shame us
when we are sexual
without wanting to be mothers,
that's why they shun us
when we speak out
or disobey their beauty standards.

They want us to be like children;
oblivious to our rights,
and satisfied with being pampered.

873.

Can we establish
that grown men
must *never* ever
call grown women
*girls*?

This infantilization
is a perpetuation
of romanticizing
females *never* growing;
*never* aging
*never* having bodily hair
*never* demanding
an equal share
*never* having loud voices
*never* objecting when others
control our choices...
*never*...
*never*...
*never* let a man
call you a *girl*, ever.


And while we're on the subject
never call girls "little women"-
let girls be girls, don't hold them up to a standard of accountability
that is bigger than them.

874.

Have you noticed
how movies, myths, and fairytales
portray
single women (who aren't loved by men)
and older women (who aren't lovable to men)
as evil????

*****

Men hate older women.

Thus older women are vilified
in every story and fairytale,
shown as ugly spinsters
and husband stealers
and whatever else evil would entail.
So that younger women
would not only despise older women
and be afraid of them
and internalize misogyny
but would also do anything in their power
to not ever be...
the older woman.
Women would seek cosmetic surgery
to defy biology
to always be young and pretty.
And in that way older women
would cease to be.
Wiped out of history.

All this, simply because

men hate older women
and men destroy anything they hate
on this earth.

Men hate older women
simply because when women are older,
we begin to fight for and understand our worth.

\*\*\*

The older I get, as a woman,
the more aware I become
of how my life has been
constructed and invested
as an object of patriarchy.

It's like waking up from a lifelong coma
and finally speaking out
finally realizing you have a voice.
Feeling your tongue lift all the weight
off your shoulders
and then, let go of it all
like a long overdue, finally paid, invoice.

That is why older women are vilified in the patriarchy,
from folklore, to myths, to children's stories
to politicians, and Hollywood movies-
the older woman is portrayed
as an evil, wicked, bitch.
Because if she is portrayed
as what she truly is

which is;
enlightened, awakened, and empowered-
the patriarchy would have died
a long time ago
and men would lose their power.

875.

Women need to stop apologizing
for being too much
for being less
for that flabby gut
for that flat chest
for being modest
for that sexy dress
for abstaining
for wanting sex
for saying no
for saying yes
for being strong
for feeling stress
for anything else
they do and become and express,
for believing they can
just like a man.
Women need to stop apologizing
for being human.

876.

Women deserve to live;
to love, to roar
to fuck, one or none
or many more,
to be the devil, to be pure
to be the virgin, to be the whore
to be modest, to be scantily clad
to be good, to be bad
to be wrong, to be right
to walk alone safely at night,
to be in heels, or flats
to be perfect, and to hell with that
to bleed, to lead,
to be child-free, to breed,
to be Eve, to be the serpent
to be Adam, to be the president,
to be heard, not just seen
to be the knight, not just the queen,
to take, not just to give.
*Women deserve to live.*
Why the fuck is it so hard to see-
that being a woman should not be
a debt,
in a world where men get
to live rent-free?


N.B. Listen to the song version of this poem; "Women Deserve To Live (Ft. Farida D.)" performed by music artist Eden Iris.

877.

How much does it cost to be a woman (and not just financially)?

Let's see;
Pink tax
Tampon tax
Period poverty
Objectified like property
Gender gap
Pay gap
Thigh gap
Tightening the vaginal gap
Orgasm gap
Virginity
Invisible hymen
Honour-killings (with a hyphen)
Slut shaming
Victim blaming
Beauty products
Bras and corsets
Painful fashion
Diet culture
Emotional labour
Unpaid labour
Childcare
Mom guilt
Having it all
Stress out of control
Dutiful daughter
Self-defence classes
Pepper spray cans
Rape whistles

Birth control pills
Abortions
IUD's
Constant checks at gynaecology
Parts of the night we never see
Rape and trauma therapy
No freedom on what to wear
and where to go,
and if you want to know
the scale of how all this holds true
just search online for #MeToo

***

It shouldn't cost a thing to be me.
It shouldn't cost a thing to have equality.

Being a woman shouldn't be
an expense.

878.

He complains about paying the tab
for the dinner date,
says that women want equality
but they won't carry the weight.

But wait.

Have you fucking seen
the tabs on a woman's plate?!

Women pay the tab for daring
to make the first move
for the hymen we must prove
for asking for sex
for wearing a mini dress
for not saying yes.

Women pay the tab for being denied
our pleasures and our rights,
told that God made us good girls
and good girls don't fight.
There is a price to pay on earth
for women to go to heaven
so we endure in silence
the scars men mark on our skins.
We pay those tabs for men
like the Jesus that died for their sins.

And then some fuckboy comes in
to measure
our desire for equality

by whether
we pay a fucking dinner tab.

When he hasn't paid a dime;
for the benefits
he enjoys via privileges
which he gets
from oppressing women
since the beginning of time.


***


Women get paid less
so men should pay more;
men should pay for the date, the movie,
and the house, and the door.

You can't be a man
who proclaims that equal pay isn't an important issue-
and then get pissed when women expect YOU to pay
for their expenses, and for your tears,
and the tissue.

879.

I'm the gold-digger?!

What are you then in the grand scheme of the bigger picture?

When you got your "gold"
from unequal pay,
and from the unpaid labour of your mother
who cooked and cleaned
and raised you up to this day.
When you run a business
that exploits and oppresses,
cheap labour
because that's the only way,
for you to hoard
all that fucking gold,
or when you run your company
making all that money
by convincing folks
to buy stuff they don't need-
you call it marketing,
(what a fancy name for greed!).
Or when the simple fact
that being a man
gives you the capital and head start
to succeed,
a system designed by men and for men
where men get the money and power
and women barter
with their beauty,
like *Beauty and the Beast*- you know that book.
Plot twist: perhaps when we "gold-dig"

we're simply taking back what you took,
from us
and then you make a fuss,
when a woman
wants to be with you
because you're well aware there's nothing
worth loving
in your scripture,
so you call her a gold-digger...

What the fuck
should we call you then
in this bigger picture???!!!

880.

If we don't depend on men-
we're spinsters.
If we do depend on men-
we're gold-diggers.

How do we win?

We don't.
Because only the patriarchy wins,
and does so by shaming us.

***

They call us 'gold-diggers'
if we depend financially on men,
but 'bitches' if we are
financially independent from them.

They call us 'desperate'
if we want love from men,
but 'spinsters' if we don't want
anything to do with them.

They call us 'sluts'
if we enjoy fucking men,
but 'prudes' if we hold back
from fucking them.

They call us 'attention seekers'
if we put effort with our looks,

but 'ugly' if we don't bother
to follow beauty books.

They call us this and that
for whatever we do
there's a tit-for-tat,
each thing has a name.
And we internalize the insults
and materialize the pain.
We find ways to change ourselves
but get hurt again.
Because they still use
different insults
to hurt us the same.

You're not free
until you realize
that you must rise
and live however you want to be.

Because you can't ever win
at a game,
where the rule is
that no matter what you do
the goal is to make you,
sink into shame.

881.

If you put effort to look pretty
they call you "attention seeker".
And if you don't put effort to look pretty
they call you "ugly".

So if I want attention I'm shamed
and if I don't care about it I'm blamed?!

                              ***


They call me "attention-seeking".

Whenever I dress in a way that
slightly stands out,
whenever I speak with a voice
that is a notch too loud-
as if I should exist with a sound
that is repeatedly receding.

But so what if I'm attention-seeking?

Your nose and your mouth
fight for the attention
of the oxygen
you're breathing.
Your tongue and your teeth
fight for the attention
of the food and water
that fills your hunger and thirst.
Even your feet,

to keep you walking,
are fighting
over who takes a step first.

So what if I'm attention-seeking?

The dead
don't fight for the attention
of oxygen-
because they are no longer breathing.

882.

He calls me a 'prude'
for wearing a long skirt,
and a 'slut'
for wearing a short one.

And if I totally strip
from the desire
to seek his validation-
he calls me a 'nasty bitch'
out of frustration,
as if his discontent
will force me again
to seek his admiration.

*** 

We're called 'sluts' if we enjoy our bodies (implying we should save our bodies).

Yet if we save our bodies we're called 'prudes' for not enjoying them (implying we should enjoy our bodies).

We can't win because the point of shaming is just to control us, by making us feel bad for whatever we decide to do.

883.

Any time a woman
stands tall in her power
whether it's in her voice
her body, her sex
her choice, her profession,
her dress-
she is called names;
*bitch, slut, whore,*
and whatever else.

Those names are used to hurt you
by breaking you down
into bits and pieces
that make you easier to devour.

But can't you see?

Those names MEAN NOTHING
other than a recognition
that you are already standing tall
in your power.

884.


Ted Yoho felt *safe* calling Alexandria Ocasio-Cortez
'a fucking bitch'
not because he thought
she won't fight back-
but because he knew
the patriarchy covers his back.

Men feel *safe* calling women
'fucking bitches'
not because they think
we won't fight back-
but because they know
the patriarchy covers their back.


*** 


We don't want an apology.
We want to dismantle the patriarchy.

As long as abusive men
are protected by a patriarchal system,
women will never be safe.

Meanwhile, let's reclaim
those sexist slurs,
because this is the way we
dismantle their power over us.

885.

The word **SLUT**
is used to degrade women
for enjoying sex.
But what's wrong with
enjoying sex?

The word **BITCH**
is used to degrade women
for being assertive.
But what's wrong with
being assertive?

Dissect the words meant to insult you.

And realize they hold no value.

886.

He labels me slutty
but he fails to see-
what's slutty is
the way he gazes,
at me.

It's not me. It's your gaze, fuckboy.

Slutty and modesty
are not found objectively
in the clothes worn
on a woman's body;
they are found in
the subjective gaze
of the male looking at
the clothes worn
on a woman's body.


That is why there is no "correct" thing to do
to avoid being sexually shamed as a woman.

The problem isn't you- it's in the gaze of the men.

887.

He labels her a 'witch'
and then people want her burnt.

He labels her a 'bitch'
and then people want her fired.

He labels her a 'slut'
and then people want her shamed.

But why doesn't anyone question
why we believe his labels
before she is blamed?

***

"Burn the witch!"
"Shame the bitch!"

Two different tactics,
two different times,
with the exact same
pitch.

N.B. Read about the Salem witch trials.

888.

She craves the kind of sex
that leaves her hair a mess,
mascara stains
on her mini dress.
She knows sixty six
positions for sex.
She has sixty six
lovers
to call an ex.
She treats them as nothing less
than a game of chess.
Sex is an experience-
*She's a bitch.*

She is a lioness
doesn't stress
to impress
she will transgress
for women's progress
and if you dare to try
to oppress
or suppress
what she wants to express
she's unafraid to grab her own pussy
to free her nipples
or to undress-
*She's a bitch*

She strives for success
a work in progress
a mother, an employee

lots of stress
yes-
attends her child's fancy dress
quickly rushes home to get ready
for her keynote address.
She works two jobs
she gets paid less
but nonetheless
she doesn't distress,
she knows what she has to offer
she knows she's excess-
*She's a bitch.*


When a woman
won't sit back and accept
the unfairness
the mess
of the sexism process,
when they expect her to be depressed
but instead
she competes with the man
she goes after what she can
what she wants to possess
and proudly confess
that she's undeterred
by the fucked up process
unafraid what people say,
that's exactly when they'll chant;
*She's a bitch.*
*She's a bitch.*
*She's a bitch.*
To interrupt
her, like it's some sort of insult

they expect her to cry as a result
of their misogynistic cult.

But she glares at them
without a glitch
because being a bitch
just means she won't flinch
she won't give in, she won't switch
her life is rich
and when they accuse her of being a witch
because how else can she endure all this?
She'll proudly chant along with them;
*I'm a bitch.*
*I'm a bitch.*
*I'm a bitch.*

This is how you reclaim,
and if your mother hadn't taught you this game
she probably hasn't realized
that this is how she, too, has survived
because every woman that has ever truly lived
is a livid
*fucking bitch.*

889.

There's not a woman I know
who hasn't been called a 'bitch'
by men she knows
and men she doesn't know.

It's part and parcel of our life
like a rites of passage we undergo.

It is a term that transcends
all cultural boundaries;
a language of bondage
a loud insult to keep us silent
within boundaries.

*Bitch.*
"What did I do to deserve it?"
You'll think, the first time you hear it.
Then you'll self-regulate
and tiptoe
wherever you go
to avoid the label
like the plague...
"He called me a bitch, but I'm not a bitch
it must be a mistake..."

And you cry. Because you buy
the shame
and it silences your outbreak.

Until one day
like an epiphany,

you decide to dissect
that word subliminally.

What does it mean to be a '*bitch*'?

My grandmother was called a 'bitch'
because she was the first in her family to go to school-
why the fuck won't she just sit
baking shit
in her kitchen
fulfilling the orders of men that rule?
*Bitch!*

My mother was called a 'bitch'
because she wanted to get a job and a purse of her own-
why the fuck won't she just
sit to be fucked
by my father at home?
*Bitch!*

I was called a 'bitch'
because I fell in love and chose my husband
instead of accept an arranged marriage
like all the women in the lineage
of my past-
how the fuck did I dare
to decide who I want to fuck
what's in my underwear
and break the system of the caste?
*Bitch!*

Take a moment to reflect
on why you're called a 'bitch'

I'd bet my life it's because you're choosing a life in which
you own your destiny; not allowing anyone tell you what to do.
Being a 'bitch' means you aren't upholding the standards of a
patriarchal system that wants to oppress you.

Being a 'bitch' is not wrong,
but the way they twisted it
into an insult is the predicament.
Because being called a 'bitch'
in this patriarchal world,
is the biggest fucking compliment.

\*\*\*

There is always a label for women
because they are always at fault.

But there are never labels for men
because they manage the settings
and configured their gender as the default.

890.

If women speak out
we are labelled 'feminists'.
When men speak out
they are just speaking out.

If women haven't had sex
we are labelled 'virgins'.
When men haven't had sex
they just haven't had sex.

If women don't want to have sex
we are labelled as 'prudes'.
When men don't want to have sex
they just don't want to have sex.

If women enjoy having sex
we are labelled 'sluts'.
When men enjoy having sex
they just enjoy having sex.

If women aren't married
we are labelled as 'spinsters'.
When men aren't married
they just aren't married.

If women are firm and assertive
we are labelled as 'bitches'.
When men are firm and assertive
they are just firm and assertive.

If women are cultivating leadership

we are labelled as 'bossy'.
When men cultivate leadership
they are just cultivating leadership.

If women are doing anything
that men are normally doing
without any label or repercussion-
they are punished by being labelled
to sentence them back into oppression.


***

.

There is no shame in who we are-
they shame us, to turn us
into who they want us to be.

Never hold on
to the shame
*they give you.*
Simply because
*it's theirs;*
it doesn't belong
to you.

891.

My mother has taught me
that when a guy says to me;
"Fuck you!" out of vice.

A simple response of;
"You wish!" would suffice.

***

When you teach girls
to be unashamed
of their voice
of their body
of their sexuality,
when they become women
no one can shame them.

892.

Shame is a box.
Insults are its locks.

They call you
a slut
a whore
a disgrace-
just to keep you in that box
when you jump out
into a free place.

But insults are words
and words have meanings
and meanings can be replaced.

When they call you a *slut*
they mean you're enjoying
your body too much-
but you must realize there is nothing
wrong with that!

When they call you a *whore*
they mean they can't keep you
under their control-
and they're not supposed to!
You ain't a child anymore!

But you know what is
truly a disgrace?
Is if their insults succeed
in keeping you

from freely exploring
this world and yourself and your place.

Don't let anybody
keep you in that box of shame.
Because the shame is when you lose
your right to life
just to win
their oppressive mind game.

*** 

Free yourself by unlearning
the shame-ridden meaning
associated with certain words, clothes, things, and expressions,
that are meant to stop you from doing things
that feel good to you, to your body, and to your self-expressions.

893.

I had to learn
early on
how to think like a man.

That they see
my body
as a sex object
that they may grab while I can't object
just because...they can.

I had to learn to look at myself
from every angle before leaving the house
to pre-think and be prepared
for what men may see
and pack a pepper spray can with me
in case things go from mild verbal abuse to something worse.
I've convinced myself that their words don't hurt...
I've had years to rehearse.

I had to learn
early on
how to think like a man,
to train
my brain
to think in reverse.

I had to learn
early on
how to think like a man,
because I was taught
that being a woman

is my curse.

894.

It is not a coincidence
that globally
the most celebrated event
for a woman
is marriage and childbirth-
in a heteronormative patriarchal world
this is the way men ensure
that they get to determine
our self-worth.


The reason
society looks down
upon
women that are
single or divorced
in a way that screams
*'oh poor you',*
is because patriarchy has enforced
the view
that a woman's value
is measured by whether
she is or isn't
loved by a man.


They call us 'witches'
and 'spinsters'
and 'bitches'
when we don't depend on men,
but 'gold-diggers' if we depend
*too much* on them.

They keep us searching for a non-existent in-between;
I know this from firsthand for I have seen
the way they look at my husband and me
because I am married, yet independent financially.
Why isn't he
"man enough" to provide for me,
and why don't I just give up my job (a.k.a. "hobby")
tend to my home and my husband
like all respectable women in society?

Fuck the patriarchy.

*Divorced?*
What a shame!
You must be that woman
that no man
wants to tame.

Don't you see how it's *always* your fault?
You are to blame!

They invent maternal instincts,
and set alarms on our biological clocks
to decide when they ring,
(men have biological clocks too-
let that fucking sink).

Getting an abortion? You'll regret it later.
Childfree by choice? You'll regret it later.

As if there is nothing greater
for you to do.
Than be a mama

to the seed of your boo.

And when you have a miscarriage
you feel like you committed the biggest sin-
society will guilt you into thinking you're in control of your womb
and the world within.

*Oh SHE IS barren!*

This patriarchal structure
keeps us locked into the roles
of wife and mother
and aspire to no other
goal.
But my darling,
I will shake your entire ancestral line until you realize
that you are not born
as just another
Matryoshka doll.

895.

As women our worth is measured
by the men we marry
by the (male) fetuses we carry;
we gain by adding on the weight of men
and by literally and figuratively
losing the weight of our body.


Our success is measured
by the amount of love
we are given by men.


Marriage is still
the most celebrated event
in a woman's history-
that a man got down on one knee
asked her "will you marry me?"
is surely
the greatest thing to happen
in a woman's life,
for she got *chosen* to be
some man's wife!


Giving birth (to a boy) is still
the most valuable purpose
for a woman's body to fulfil,
to bring an heir
is her ticket to secure
her husband's will.
Female infanticide is still a thing
yet abortions are frowned upon
because you could kill,

a potential male.

I'll rob those double standards-
take me to fucking jail!

Our success is measured
by the amount of love
we are given by men,
warped and ingrained and fed to us
as a fairytale.

Our success is measured
by the amount of love
we are given by men.
As if being loved by men
is the greatest achievement
for women.

                         ***


Then again,
perhaps being loved by men
is an achievement
in a world full of misogyny.
And since feminism is fighting
to liberate women from the
validation of that love,
feminists are seen as the tyranny.

896.

The patriarchy
has women convinced
that being loved
is the reason we exist-
to the extent
that even as we fight
the patriarchy,
we seek to be loved
by the enemy.


\*\*\*


Don't talk back.
Don't be loud.
Men don't want a woman
that is proud.
Don't be too slutty.
Don't be too prudish.
Men don't like a woman
"too" much of this.
Don't be independent.
Don't be a gold-digger.
Men don't feel manly when drained
or when a woman pulls the trigger.
Don't be too thin.
Don't be too fat.
Men aren't turned on
by either of that.
Don't be a feminist.
Don't be a doormat.

Men want you to have rights
but only the rights they give you.
Don't challenge this
or else no man would love you.

And for a lifetime women live
with those unspoken rules,
pass them on to our daughters
like a pair of used shoes
that don't fit
but they still wear it
never mind the blisters
never mind the splinters
never mind if it cut into their feet
like a pair of scissors,
never mind if they never ran...

As if the worst thing that can ever happen to a woman
is to not be loved by a man.

***

Men hate women
who do not conform.

They hate us
when we say what we want
when we do what we want
when we wear what we want;
they hate us in accordance.
Because men never loved us

what they love
is our conformance.

897.

I don't want a man
who treats me like a queen.

"You don't need to go to work" he says
"I'll go work double instead- I promise I'll treat you like a queen".

"You don't need to leave the house" he says
"I'll get you everything you need- I promise I'll treat you like a
queen".

"You don't need an income" he says
"What's mine is yours- I promise I'll treat you like a queen".

And to the naive me it would seem
that treating me like a queen
means living right out of
my favourite love movie scene,
but in fact, treating me like a queen
means I am a prisoner
dependant on a man
for the most basic necessities
and the extra luxuries
and everything in between.
So that if one day he turns out to be an asshole of a king
I will struggle to give him back his ring,
because I cannot survive
without a job or an income of my own,
his castle isn't actually my home.
I've seen this happen far too many times,
a woman depends on a man she loves
and then he turns into a monster

but she ignores all the signs
he's got her to confine
because she has nowhere else to dine.
So carefully read the following lines:

I want a job and an income
and I'll get my own stuff done,
before we start fucking
let this be foreseen;
I want equality-
I don't want a man
who treats me like a queen.

\*\*\*

The Master
who treats
his slaves well,
is still a Master.

898.

Don't do to me
the things you see
in porn.

I was not born,
to star
as an object
in your sexual fantasy.

I don't want you to gag me
to choke me
to fuck me
like a hammer bangs a nail.
I don't want to fake my happy ending
for the happy ending
of your porn fairytale.

What you see in porn
doesn't turn me on
it turns me into an object.
I have sexual desires
and boundaries you must respect.

I am not a prude
because I don't like sex to be dehumanizing and rough.

I am not boring
because I don't want to make porn
out of the way we make *love*.

Unlearn what you have normalized

to be a turn on
instead
of bringing all your misogyny
into our bed.

\*\*\*

There are women who like to be choked during sex,
and there are women who don't.

There are women who like dirty talk during sex,
and there are women who don't.

There are women who like anal sex,
and there are women who don't.

What you do with one woman
is not an open invitation to try on
every other woman you're with.
Surprise; different women have different desires,
we aren't a monolith.

899.

I learned what men like
by watching porn,
but that's also how I learned
to ignore what I like.


\*\*\*


Only in porn
everybody orgasms
at the same time.
In real life
each body
has its own rhyme.


\*\*\*


Heterosexual men think *sex*
begins with their boners
and ends with their orgasms.


But that's *masturbation*.


It's not sex
unless your partner is also wet
ends with you in a spasm.

900.

Imagine during sex
I just focus on your balls
because that's where your
reproduction ability falls.
Imagine that it's ingrained
in every woman's brain
to value you, just for your testes
even if they're not having sex with you
with the goal of having kids.
Imagine this;
I somehow convince you
too,
that pleasure is only experienced
in your testes;
not your base, not your shaft,
not your glans, not your foreskin.
Imagine if no woman has ever
touched your balls
I'd call you a 'virgin'.
Imagine if sex
was just about your balls;
because that's what you do to women
when you make sex just about
our vaginal holes.

*** 

My vagina is not a rabbit hole
for you to plough

out of control.

There is a maze
if you zone out of your penetrative male gaze
you'll see-
that it's not just a vaginal hole,
I have an entire vulva anatomy.

If you want to please me
stop seeing me as a hole.

Exploring the maze is more fun
than heading straight to the door.


My clitoris
is the doorbell
to my vagina.

If you can't find it, and ring it,
you're not coming in.

I am not
a highway inn.

*** 


In sex women need to be selfish;
because no one will look out for our best interest.
We must say 'yes' when we want to get pleasure
and say 'no' when we don't want to give consent.

901.

I open the door
of my legs
to reveal a maze.

A Sudoku puzzle
a snakes and ladders, staircase.

To climb up to my orgasm
or to heaven
(it's the same thing),
you need to know, before you enter
which bells to ring.

A little to the left.
A little to the right.
And I just might,
show you how a woman
turns into a werewolf,
under your full
moonlight.

I open the door
of my legs
to reveal a maze.

You want to rush into the entrance-
but if you find the keys first,
I'll lock you in for days.

***

This whole idea
that the clitoris
is
so hard to find,
is a conspiracy
made up by men
who don't know how to
please women.

902.

"Are you sure there isn't another hole??"

He asked almost losing his mind-
he didn't know my period comes out
of the same hole he likes to grind.

"Oh wait let me check-
you're right!" I told him,
"there's a hole for my blood
a hole for my hymen,
a hole for my shit
a hole for my pee,
a hole for my clit,
a hole for my baby
and a special hole right there
just for you
to fuck me!"

"Phew" he said,
"you had me doubting my knowledge
of female anatomy!"


N.B. True story.

903.

STOP CALLING MY VULVA
A VAGINA.

The vagina is the opening
where sperm enters, and babies exist,
and where menstrual blood would shed.

But you must learn about the vulva
if you want to please
a vagina-owner in bed.

It is the patriarchy
that reduces me to an object
for penetration and pregnancy,
negating my pleasure as unnecessary-
so they refer to my vulva
as a vagina instead.

***

The patriarchy has normalized
calling female genitals *vagina*
(instead of *vulva*)
to not only focus the sexual discourse
only on heterosexual male pleasure,
but to also normalize the mutilation
of female pleasure from sex.

The vagina is just the part of our genitals that is relevant for penetration.

The vulva is our entire external female genitals which includes (but not limited to) our vaginal opening.

N.B. Recommended reading: *Practicing 'psychic genital mutilation'* by Harriet Lerner (www.chicagotribune.com)

904.

During sex
men are taught to focus on
*feeling* good,
while women are taught to focus on
*looking* good.

From sex education, to the porn industry
to lingerie stores-
the goal is to turn women into nets
where men can score.

That is why
men know exactly *what*
pleases them in bed,
while women know exactly *how*
to fake an orgasm instead.

\*\*\*

I actually deserve an Oscar
for the number of times I've acted out
a fake orgasm.

It takes talent
to moan and rock,
and spasm
and narrate that it's
the "best fuck",
all in tandem.

It takes skill
to ignore the fact
that men ignore my pleasure,
and to memorize
the script of the sex act
down to each letter;
the show begins
with their erections
and ends
when their sperm makes a splatter.

But most of all
I deserve that Oscar
for the number of times I've truly believed,
that my orgasm
doesn't matter.

\*\*\*

Imagine,
if women had to orgasm
to get pregnant.
The human race
would lose the race.

N.B. The Orgasm Gap.

905.

We know for sure that we are here
because a man ejaculated,
but we don't know for sure whether
the womb that carried us has consented.

How many of us are here
because of
broken condoms
broken vows,
broken laws
of abortion ploughs?

I wonder.

I know I'm here
because my father
had a moment of pleasure.

But I wonder.

What about my mother?

\*\*\*

Every person on this earth
exists because a man
had a moment of pleasure-
we know that much to be true.

But how many of us exist
because a woman
had an orgasm too?

906.

I look at my son,
and I believe in the *Big Bang*.


For this is how he came into the world;
his father was *Big*
and I was *Banged*.

907.

I asked for sex.

I didn't ask for the condom to break
I didn't ask to pay for a man's "honest" mistake.

Why can a man have sex
without any consequence,
while I pay the price of his orgasm
from my expense?


\*\*\*



We live in a world where
we don't punish men for sexual violence,
but we punish women for consensual sex;
by shaming their pleasure
by banning abortions
by forcing them to be mothers.


Oh why are women made to suffer?!

908.

Some men
treat women
like a gym sock;
they release their load in them
but deny them
the right to consent
the right to pleasure
the right to abortion.

Some men
are living in a distortion.


They just want to have sex with us-
and they don't want
to wear condoms,
and they also don't want
women's birth control
to be accessible for all,
but what they do want
is for abortions to be illegal.

They just want to have sex with us-
and they want us
to live in the times
of the medieval.

They just want to have sex with us-
and they want us
to only ever want
to be mothers,
(otherwise we're evil).

They just want to have sex with us-
and they want sex
for them, to be about pleasure
for us, to be about consequence.

But our wombs aren't factories
and our lives aren't an expense.
So if they just want to have sex with us
we also *just* want to have sex,
with nothing more than a moment's pleasure
(and certainly nothing less).


N.B. Thousands in Poland protest against near-total abortion ban
which went into effect January 2021.

909.

Isn't it ironic that
the men who protest against abortion
aren't also protesting against pleasure
as an *end goal* in sex?

It's almost as if they want pleasure
but they want only women
to pay for their sperm's consequence.


I'm going to boycott having sex
with men, who are anti-abortion;
because why the fuck should I
give you the right to enjoy my body,
when you believe I should not only
have no rights over my body,
but also that I should pay my life
for the consequences of YOUR body
in a moment of pleasure?

I am a human; not a disposable cup
to be tossed at your leisure.

I don't know if you were told this
by anyone else;
but I won't pay my life
for your 3 minutes of sex.


***

Once you deposit your semen
inside a vagina-
it's checkmate.
That semen is no longer yours
to determine its fate.

910.

"If women didn't have casual sex
abortions won't be needed!"
he said.

So I said;
"If men didn't have casual
abortions won't be needed!"

***

The cause of an unwanted pregnancy is not
sex outside of marriage,
sex inside of marriage,
sex with multiple partners,
sex with one partner,
or an egg that swims to a sperm.

The cause of an unwanted pregnancy is
a sperm that swims to an egg.

So if you absolutely
need to regulate-
it makes more sense,
to regulate sperm
before its consequence,
in the womb.

We can effectively reduce
the abortion rate
not by criminalizing abortion;
but by criminalizing
the heterosexual intercourse
of men who are against abortion.

Snip it in the bud buddy.

911.

Sometimes
you're taking all precautions,
you wear gloves and a mask
and you sanitize
and you sing 'happy birthday'
as you wash your hands,
and you STILL
get the Coronavirus.

Sometimes
you're taking all precautions,
you wear a condom and are on the pill
and you STILL
get accidently pregnant.

Why is that hard for people
to understand?

\*\*\*

Believing that
birth control is the solution
to eliminate abortion,
is like believing that
life jackets are the solution
to eliminate drowning.

Sometimes the life jacket malfunctions.

Sometimes the life jacket is forgotten.

Sometimes someone pushes you into the water;
and you don't have a chance to get your life jacket,
or you don't own a life jacket because you don't go in the water
anyway,
or you don't even know how to swim (let alone use a life jacket).

And sometimes
everything is perfectly in place
you know how to swim
your life jacket is on
the weather is great,
but an unexpected tide
writes out your fate,
knocks off your breath,
and despite all the precautions you took
you end up suffocated.

So before you say "birth control is the solution to eliminate abortion"
make sure you're fucking educated.

912.

When our hunter-gatherer
ancestors
decided to become farmers
and settle down,
it led to a boom in births
because they spent more time fucking
fertile wombs,
instead of wandering around plucking
fertile grounds.
And while the women were busy
with a cycle of pregnancy, childbearing, rearing, and more pregnancy,
men took over ownership and management of the farming property.

Women were reduced to sex objects
valued only for reproduction.
Men had all sorts of future prospects
for they owned all forms of production-
and this included owning
the women who were used
to create more children;
the girls followed their mother's destiny
and the boys were given,
their father's succession.

From this inequality
came the birth of the patriarchy.

And if you know this history,
you will not only know
the patriarchy's origin;
but you will also understand why

the men who uphold patriarchy
are so against abortion.


\*\*\*


A woman
who controls
the destiny of her womb,
controls
the destiny of her life.

That is why men are so invested
with restricting our abortion rights-
they want to control
the destiny of our lives.

913.

If women are expected
to justify an abortion
of a fetus they didn't want,
then men must justify
their ejaculation
in a womb that didn't want.


***


People think abortion
is only viable
if a woman was raped
or if she has a medical condition.

Let me break this to you,
this is a list of other viable reasons for abortion too:
-I'm not ready to be a mother
-I don't want to be a mother
-I am a mother and can't afford more kids
-I am a mother and don't want more kids
-I control my body and my life.

Women
are allowed
to leave
a legacy
that is about
more than what
they can create

with sperm and eggs.

Women
are not
baby-making machines
with legs.

If you say only rape or medical conditions
qualify women for abortions,
you're saying that for a woman to be allowed
to control her body
and her life,
she must first go through trauma
and prove that she can survive.

Abortions are essential healthcare, they are not a prize.

*** 

I exist
because my mother
had a choice;
I will always be
pro-choice.

914.

You say I'm selfish
for getting an abortion.

You want me punished.

So selfishness,
for a woman, is a crime?

I dare you to name all the selfish men who are ruling our world,
without paying time.

\*\*\*

You say;
What if the fetus
would be
the next president
but couldn't
because you determined
its fate?

I say;
What if the woman
forced to carry the fetus
would be
the next president
but couldn't
because you determined
her fate?

If the life of the would-be matters
but the life of the living woman
doesn't matter-
then it's not a *pro-life* debate.


The question of whether a fetus is a person
is up for debate.

The question of whether a woman is a person
should not be up for debate.


\*\*\*


So abortions are wrong
but female foeticide is okay?
So then abortions are wrong
only because
the fetus might be
a male one day?!


N.B. Female foeticide is the practice of aborting fetuses for the sole
reason of being identified as female.

915.

"ABORTION IS MURDER!"
they yell,
"THE LIFE IN YOUR WOMB
IS A LIFE ON ITS OWN
AND IT IS NOT YOUR LIFE
TO DECIDE TO END IT!"

Let's take that logic
and truly comprehend it.

If the life in my womb
is a life on its own;
why is it using my body
as a home?

Take it out!
Let's see
if you can make it survive alone
without ME!

This life you're talking about
cannot be sustained without
MY LIFE.

This life you're talking about
suckles from my own blood
and bone
to build a life of its own,
without me it cannot live-
it gets a life
only from

the life I give.

Next time someone tells you
the life in the womb is a life on its own,
tell them to take the clump of cells
and give it a home
that is outside of a uterus
and outside of a woman's life, blood, and bone.


If you think a fetus
is a separate entity-
take it out of the uterus
and let it survive separately!


***


The irony?

A fetus is treated
as an independent body
with its own independent rights-
yet the woman creating it
still fights
for her own independent rights!

916.

If the fetus in my womb
is a person already
and I am its sole incubator;
I demand its full rights now
because...why wait 9 months later?

It's a person already
so I have given it a name.
Thus I need its I.D. card processed immediately
and a passport with a visa to Spain.
It needs a holiday from all the hard work
it's doing (all by itself)
to grow a heart and a brain.

I also need to claim
all governmental
child benefits and support.
That kid has taken a mortgage
to use my womb as a fort.

I need to enrol it at nursery school-
don't tell me the slots are reserved
for kids outside the uterus!
My child is a person already
stop treating it as if it's worthless!

I also need a maternity leave
starting from the day of conception.
Add in a few extra days
because those ultrasounds
just give a prediction.

Farida D.

I mean I'm already a mother
since the fetus inside,
is already a child.

The fetus in my body
is demanding its rights
and if you deny it those rights
until it is actually born
for its existence to be certain;
tell me why do you keep preaching
that a fetus in the womb
is already a person?!

917.

They show you the sonogram
a lump of cells twitching
electric waves swimming,
that they tell you is a heartbeat.
They show you
to convince you
that abortion is a murderous feat.
But I wonder how you would feel
if they showed you what's real
outside the screen of clumpy cells
and inside a heart that actually swells.
What if
instead of showing you a *potential* life
they show you the *actual* life
of the women down your local street.
The women forced into motherhood, or unsafe abortions,
or dead by the defeat.
I wonder how you would feel
if they told you what's real;
that pro-life means that *just your life* as a woman
can never be called shotgun-
you're always in the backseat.

*** 

When you legalize abortions
you don't increase foetal mortality-
you decrease maternal mortality.

N.B. Every 8 minutes a woman in a developing nation will die of complications arising from an unsafe abortion. (Source: World Health Organization).

918.

Denying a woman from abortion
is like denying a man from releasing
his sperm into anything other than
a fertile womb
and only for the purpose
of reproduction.

919.

Why are men
letting their sperm
purposely die
by tugging it out of
their penises
while masturbating,
when that sperm can
potentially form a life?!

*MURDERERS!*

I need to sit you down and explain
the seriousness of this loss
and the utter disdain;
what if that sperm
you purposely
washed down your drain,
could have been
the next Beethoven?
Or the one who would solve
our climate crisis?
What if that sperm
would end the pandemic
of the Coronavirus?!
This is THE reason
why God says
masturbation is a sin!

*Shame on you
for not obeying Him!*

And what about all the men
who struggle with low sperm
production, erectile dysfunction,
and infertility?
While you're here insensitively practically
throwing your sperm around like confetti!

*What a pity!*

By the way,
your selfishness is not only
killing so many potential lives-
it's also destroying women's dreams
to be mothers,
instead of just being wives!

N.B. If we use pro-life logic to talk to men the way we talk to women
about abortions.

920.

Seriously,
if abortion is murder;
then how come
male masturbation
isn't *manslaughter*?!


If abortion is murder,
then male ejaculation
as a result of masturbation
is murder too.
How many of those sperms
could have been
the next president,
or a Nobel prize winner,
or the greatest inventor ever...?
Those sperms missed their chance for life
because a man selfishly stroked them
out of his erect cock;
and instead of giving them life in a womb
he buried them into a sock.

If abortion is murder,
then men are murderers
for masturbating
or even having
a casual fuck.

If abortion is murder,
then female ovulation
that ends with menstruation

is murder too.
But while this process can't be helped
when it comes to masturbation
men can surely do.

If abortion is murder,
where do we draw the line?
Why is it only when sperm meets egg
that it becomes a crime?
If a fetus is alive
before it meets life-
then sperm and egg
are alive
before they form a fetus.

And if all this
sounds like nonsense-
I want to remind you
that this is the basis
of the argument for *pro-life*.

921.

According to
Jeremiah 1:5 **"Before I formed you in the womb I knew you..."**
this verse is used by Christians to support the argument for pro-life.

So let's just simply follow this logic
without any arguments or strife;

If God knew you before forming you in the womb
it means he knew the part of you
outside the womb,
which technically speaking
is the sperm.

Thus, male masturbation is a rightful concern.

When men masturbate
or ejaculate
outside a womb-
they are killing sperms
which could form a potential life.

Male masturbation becomes manslaughter,
because it doesn't result
in a son or a daughter.


"You can't say male masturbation is akin to manslaughter", they tell
me,
"because this means any ejaculation outside the womb is
manslaughter-
it means sex can't be JUST for pleasure!"

"Exactly!"
I say
"according to religion
sex should be,
between a married man and woman,
to procreate together.
What the fuck is all this new-age nonsense
about sex being for pleasure?!"

They pause as their logic brings potential disaster. The devil bursts
into laughter.

They say:
"So is ejaculating in a condom
while having sex with *only your wife*-
also manslaughter
of a potential life?"

"Duh- yes", I tell them
"in fact so many religions
ban or prohibit birth control
even declare it a sin-
because you are attempting to stop God
from planting a life within
the womb of a woman".

"Then based on that logic,
what about non-heterosexual sex?"
they say,
"is it wasting potential life, because it can't create life anyway?"

"You know that this is true",

I walk the religious logic through,
"religion isn't exactly ecstatic
about non-heterosexual sex
for that reason too!"

They pause. The devil and his mates give me a standing ovation and
applause.

"So what about periods then?" they continue with strife,
"if an unfertilized egg leaves your body
did you just kill a potential life?"

"No not really" I explain,
"although at the outset it sounds the same-
but you can't control periods
yet you can control not tugging a penis
deliberately,
until you purposely,
kill a potential life.
Periods are God's will- but God is clear that masturbation is a sin.
All I'm saying is men must abstain".

They say;
"Sperm cells will die and renew anyway
if not ejaculated!"
So I tell them;
"Then let them die on their own instead of being a murderer
because you masturbated!"

They look at me with utter disdain,
and sheer horror

realizing they're murderers if they ever,
masturbate again.

"That's all insane",
they bring the conversation back to the starting point,
"if God knew you before he formed you in the womb;
then God knew which sperm will make it to the womb
and which sperm will be masturbated down the drain".

"I agree!" I say ecstatically,
"and following that same
logical conclusion;
if God knew which sperm will make it to the womb
then God knows which sperm will be an abortion!"

They pause, as I continue to clear their distortion;
"Following the pro-life logic
if God knows which sperm will be given life
then God also knows which sperm he will kill-
thus continuing a pregnancy or ending it with abortion,
are both God's predetermined will".

922.

"You should be flattered" he says
each time he ejaculates
after 2.59 minutes of sex.

"It's because you're so sexy" he would go into an elaboration
as he pretends to not see my frustration.

He fucking expects from me appreciation
for the fact that when *we*
have sex
only *he*
is having fun.

He thinks sexy women
are for him to use;
it doesn't matter
if they didn't cum.

923.

Let me tell you about the way I like to have sex-
don't shove all my hard work
of paperwork
and plump me on my desk
rip my clothes off and grab my chest,
this type of porn movie sex
translates to real life stress.
I worked hard all day, please don't turn it into a mess
I can't get turned on while you're fucking
up my desk
or ruining my favourite dress.

Let me tell you about the way I like to have sex-
whisper sweet nothings in my ear
call me dear
with the honey of your tongue,
hold my hands, pull me near
listen to my heart beat
like it's your favourite song.

Ask me, what I'd like
tell me, what you'd like.


Take your time to run
your fingers all over me
slowly,
like your dick is on strike.


Consent before pleasure.
Because only consent leads to pleasure.

It may come as a surprise
but I don't enjoy being eaten
(but I do like to eat)-
perhaps because men have been
gobbling me like salami
while I suck them like a sweet.

I, too, am a treat.

I'm open- if you want to try.
But I have to warn you
that my hopes aren't particularly high.

Trail your fingers up my thigh
then go back to whispering
another lullaby.

Let's pause...

to pour some wine

It's only half past nine.

Tease me like there is no end to time.

Let's talk some more.

Let's make love to poetry
like the sea does to the shore.

Sex isn't a game or a competition; we don't have to rush to the score.

I am a woman,
sex with me is a trip to heaven
not a grocery store
chore.

I will finally be ready and wet,
after your dick has gone up and down
and up and down and up and down
like a roller coaster
and now at a standstill firmly erect.

Push it in me
gently,
lock the seatbelt.

Let's pump up the ride,
from our anticipation and sweat.

Keep going. Slower and faster.
We're on that roller coaster
and we're feeling our hearts rise high.

Don't ask me if I'm close,
for when I am, you'll feel my soul in the sky.

This is the way I like to have sex.

And sometimes, if you let me know beforehand, to lock my important
documents away-
I won't mind
if you mess up my desk
and fuck me like a stamp on payday!

924.

I love morning sex
while we're both alert and aware
of one another.
Not drunken night sex
where we just move along the motions
of how we're supposed to be lovers.

I love random sex.

I love sex that breaks the rules
of what I'm supposed to like;
missionary, compulsory
whenever and whatever
my husband would like.

Fuck that.

Fuck me at random.

Fuck me when I want it to happen,
in every position
with every star
that goes to sleep.

Rub my clit in circles
until I see the circle
of life-
until my clit feels too dizzy
for me to stand upright.

I don't like it rough.

The tip of your dick, for now, is enough.

I prefer making love,
in every place on my body
before we land in my vagina.

Mark me like a map;
it takes time to travel
from America to China.

Love me softly;
like the dawn that stretches slowly
filling up the morning sky.

I love morning sex
because I can see
you... and you and I.

*** 

A woman enjoying being a submissive
in a consensual BDSM context
is not misogyny.

Misogyny is when we expect
women to not have kinks of their own.

925.

Sometimes
I love to masturbate on my own
even when my husband is right there at home,
and we
can technically
have sex together-
but I just enjoy
learning how to
love myself better.

I go to the next room
lie my body down alone
on clouds of pillows
until I get wetter.

Sometimes I don't want sex for two,
not that sex with my husband isn't amazing too-
but I have no explanation as to why
sometimes, I just want sex for one.

It is not a sin is it, to have fun?

926.

Sisters.
Mothers.
Aunts.

Brothers.
Fathers.
Uncles.


The betrayal cuts deep.
I can't wake up
from the nightmare
that won't let me sleep.

You held me down.

Ripped the sparkle of my crown.

For a future husband, you mutilated my genitals
For man you haven't even met,
you nip my sexual organs
believing I'll be pure when I can't get wet.

You all betrayed me.

Don't tell me that you love me,
when you clearly love
misogyny.


\*\*\*

They mutilated
my pleasure
because
as a woman
as a female
I am expected to be
sexually
available for men
but if I felt pleasure from them
then I was a slut.
I must not
feel pleasure
but just be pleasurable.
Because men are afraid
that if I enjoy sex too much
I'll go ride every dick I see,
because that's what men do
to other women
and to me.


N.B. Female genital mutilation (FGM) involves the partial or total removal of external female genitalia for the belief that this reduces libido and thus curbs sexual desire of girls and women. More than 200 million girls and women alive today have been cut in 30 countries in Africa, the Middle East, and Asia, despite the fact that it is internationally recognized as a violation of human rights. (Source: World Health Organization).

927.

The sexual act
is viewed in the patriarchy
as something that
females *give* while males *take*.


The *giver* gains nothing
the *taker* gets everything.


The *giver* ends up with nothing left
while the *taker* gets it all.


The *giver* thus becomes weaker
while the *taker* has full control.

928.

We frame sex as a subtraction for women.
We frame sex
as something that women *give away*;
we tell them that they
*lose* their virginity
the first time they do it.
And the more they *give* sex
the more they *lose* parts of their modest selves.
And the more and more
they *give* and *lose*,
the more and more
they deduce
and reduce
their self-worth
until they're not,
respectable women
but instead "sluts".


We frame sex as an addition for men.
We frame sex
as something that men *take away*;
we tell them that they
*gain* experience
the first time they do it.
And the more they *take* sex
the more they *gain* parts of their masculine selves.
And the more and more
they *take* and *gain*,
the more and more
they deduce

and induce
their self-worth
until they begin to bud,
from being just men
to being desirable "studs".


***


Women *lose* their virginity
but men, *score*.

Men can enjoy sex,
but if a woman does
she's obviously a *whore*.

This mentality
not only hurts women
but does so much more.

It teaches women that sex
is something they 'give away'.
The concept of *whoreness*
assumes your value fades away
the more sex you have
as if your worth
can be deduced
from a numerical measure.

While as for men, it teaches them
not only that sex is their right
but it begins with their boners,

and ends with their pleasure.

How can we have equality
in the bedroom
when sex is viewed
as a male-only leisure?


When women are viewed as "givers" of sex
we "save" ourselves
for the right one,
and then we "lose" our virginity.
For the rest of our lives
we "give" and "withhold" sex
like a reward and penalty
like a prize or punishment to our partners for their behaviour,
we master the art of giving blowjobs
and give our own orgasms a waiver.

If we enjoy "taking" sex, we're called *sluts*.
If we refuse to "give" sex, we're called *prudes*.

Because we are made by patriarchy to be "givers",
men assume the role of "takers".

A man who enjoys "taking" sex is called a *stud*.
He keeps track of his *score-*
it's higher when he "takes" more.
When he comes, he believes the sex act is done,
so he turns around to snore.

If he is denied sex by a woman,
he complains about being "friend-zoned".

He rapes (not because that red mini-skirt is a bullfight flag)
but because he believes he's "owed"
the right to *take* sex.
He blames it on women if he's an incel.

Our world suffers from the inability to understand "consent"
because we struggle to implement
equality in sex.

Both consenting partners should give and take;
and sex shouldn't be anything less.

929.

There is something
so fucking uncomfortable
about when my man
sneaks up behind me
to fondle me, touch me,
without asking me
while I'm clearly busy
doing something else,
just helping himself to me
thinking his entitlement
is him behaving
romantically.


If you think
I'm just a pretty
static, inanimate object
that you can just grab
out of the blue-
perhaps I should cut off your balls
to show you that I'm not static;
I can perform things without asking for your consent too.

930.

Men seem to always
want to play that game
where I say 'stop'
and they keep going
and they keep ignoring
my plea
as if when I say 'stop'
I mean it as a challenge
and they will take no defeat.


How can I tell them
that every woman
that ever said 'stop'
said it because she already
feels defeated?

You won.

Now can you 'stop'?
Because I'm too tired to run.


***


Saying "no" softly doesn't mean
keep pushing me for a "yes".
It means I'm fucking scared
that you'll get aggressive
if I get assertive.

931.

"BUT I'M SO CLOSE. I'M ALMOST COMING"

is NEVER the correct response
when she tells you to stop fucking.
Sex is not a race;
that begins with your boner
and must end with your orgasm,
for you to be winning.
Sex is a ladder;
each step requires consent
and just because you started climbing
don't mean that consent,
is no longer relevant-
you need to keep checking.

I don't care how close you are to coming.
You can't just ignore my discomfort and keep going.

932.

Let's normalize
the idea that
safe sex
includes
consent
as much as
it includes
condoms.

933.

When you make plans with friends,
you can still change your mind about going.

When you start playing a game with others,
you can still change your mind about playing.

When you reach the cashier at the store,
you can still change your mind about purchasing.

When you start having sex,
you can still change your mind about continuing.

Whatever the reason, whatever you're doing,
you are allowed to change your mind about pursuing.

934.

Imagine you're really thirsty
and you go get some water
and people shame you
for having so much.
Ridiculous, right?

Now imagine you're not thirsty
and you don't go get some water
and people shame you for that too.
Ridiculous, right?

Now imagine you ask for some water
because you just want a sip
and people force you to have all of it.
Ridiculous, right?

Now imagine you ask for some water
then change your mind about it,
and people force you to have all of it.
Ridiculous, right?

Now imagine you don't ask for water
but someone assumes you look thirsty
so they pour water all over you
and as you drown,
people say well you looked thirsty
or you asked for water last time in town.
Ridiculous, right?

Now imagine you replace the words.
'thirsty' with 'horny'

and 'water' with 'sex'.
Ridiculous, right?!

935.

I was at a Lebanese restaurant
and as the waiter
took my food order
he began to forcefully convince me
to change my mind about what I was ordering to eat
and instead get another dish with kebab meat.

I kept saying I'd rather get something else
and he kept hearing my "no" as a "push for a yes"
and he kept pushing towards my defeat.

I got the dish he suggested
I hated it
and I ended up paying for something
I did not even eat.

But more alarmingly
I couldn't help but wonder
if that's how he treats a customer,
how does he then treat,
the women
he takes to his bedroom
when they say "no" to his meat?

936.

You are never obligated
to say "yes".

Saying "yes"
is not a debt
that women must pay
to the men who are nice to us,
simply because they are nice to us.

Lack of consent is not the price
we must pay for basic human decency.

Men must be nice to us,
and they must be nice for free.

937.

Consent is the seed of equality;
it births a win-win situation for all parties.

When we start by planting consent in the bedroom
(because that's where most of us are formed),
we normalize taking that seed with us into every other room;
into our schools, our workplaces, entertainment, and court rooms,
into our relationships and interactions-
understanding violations and sanctions
setting and respecting boundaries
not hurting ourselves or anybody.

Understanding consent
is not just about sex;
it is about making the world
safe for everybody.

938.

We can strip off our clothes
but we cannot strip off our privileges
in the bedroom.

There is still a power dynamic
in our ability to consent
to how we take things further.
And if we don't see it,
we risk hurting one another.

\*\*\*

**Privilege and consent in sex:**

We must understand privilege to understand consent in sexual
partnerships. When there is an imbalance of privilege in a sexual
partnership (whether it's gender, status, race, age, etc), the oppressed
partner's ability to freely consent is immediately jeopardized because
they are accustomed and conditioned to say 'yes' to those who hold
privilege (or else suffer consequences). If you are the privileged
partner in a sexual partnership, always ask your partner(s) whether
they are consenting because they genuinely *want to*, or consenting
because they feel they *have to*. And then use that awareness to act
with care.

939.

How to understand consent (simply):

Is it your body?
Yes--> Help yourself to it.
No--> Ask.

*** 

The first lesson of consent
comes not from another respecting
the boundaries of our body.
It comes from us respecting
the boundaries of our body.

Are you listening
to what your body is saying?
Are you giving it what it asks for?
Stopping when it says "no more"?
Or are you treading on it
showing others how to trample on it
like a 'welcome' mat on the floor?

Our bodies are always talking to us
we are its protectors all along.
When we listen to what it needs
we won't ever get it wrong.

Stop what you're doing now.

Ask your body what it needs

and actually listen.

That is the first lesson.

When you learn to hear your body
you won't tolerate those who won't listen.

940.

When I was a kid
my aunt used to tell me
that if I don't finish
all the food on my plate
God will punish me
for wasting.

And so, even when I was full
I would force myself to keep eating.

When I got married
my aunt told me
that if I don't satisfy my husband sexually
whenever he wanted it
God will punish me
for hesitating.

And so, even when I was not in the mood,
I would force myself to keep fucking.


Consent isn't just about sex;
it is an attitude and a willingness
to self-respect and expect respect
for the limits of your body.

***

They tell you
don't sit alone with a strange man
because that's the recipe for rape.
Men have only one thing
on their mind
and you aren't strong enough to escape.

And then they arrange your marriage
to a strange man
and they tell you it's okay he's your husband.
Your husband can't rape you
because your husband *has a right* to have sex with you.

They think rape comes only from
a man who has *no right*
to have sex with you.

They think it is *not rape* when they say
your husband *has a right*
to have sex with you.

941.

Dear Girls,
They say
you are made of
sugar AND spice;
which means saying NO
is just as important
as being nice.

\*\*\*

Dear Women,
Don't believe anyone
who tells you otherwise.
Fuck the sugar, embrace the spice.
Saying NO
is always safer for you
than being nice.

942.

There are fairytales
that teach girls
to get a prince
they must first kiss
a frog.
And there are fairytales
that teach boys
to get a princess
they must first kiss
her while she's asleep.

Do you realize how deep
those fairytales seep?

There are women
who believe
it's their job to fix
and nurture a fuckboy.
And there are men
who believe
consent isn't applicable
to what they enjoy.

\*\*\*

It's not enough
to teach your girls
to say "no".
You must also
teach your boys

to understand "no".


And if we teach girls to say "no"
(instead of pleasing others),
and if we teach boys that they aren't entitled
(instead of being served by their mothers)-
consent wouldn't be so hard to understand when they're adults,
and victims will be empowered to see
that it is never their fault.

943.

He says:
"So if you like the guy hitting on you- it's sexy
but if you don't like him- it's harassment?
That doesn't make sense!"

So I interrupt his nonsense:
"It does!
But only if you understand
the basic principle of consent!"

***

Consent is simple- why can't you see?
It just means
I make the choice for myself
instead of you making the choice for me.

944.

I was once with a guy
who told me
"I care about consent
and I want you to know
that I consent to touching you".

I stared at him blankly.

For a century
or two.

Can being delusional
be any more
true?

N.B. I always have a choice to consent, but my consent is never your choice.

945.

Going back to your place
is not consent to anything other than
going back to your place.

If you think going back to your place
means you can now fuck me-
let me ask you
how many houses have you agreed to go to,
where your presence wasn't taken to mean
that anyone can now stick their dick in you?!

946.

'Yes' to a date is not a 'yes'
to sex.

'Yes' to a drink is not a 'yes'
to sex.

'Yes' to a kiss is not a 'yes'
to sex.

And even a 'yes' to sex is not a 'yes'
*to all* sex.

\*\*\*

Let's normalize the notion
that consent to sex
is NOT inclusive of
consent to sexual fetishes.

Consent to sex
and consent to sexual fetishes
are two DIFFERENT things.

947.

Let's normalize
rightly asking
for consent,
instead of
consenting
to what's wrongly
been normalized.

\*\*\*

*Beauty and the Beast*
is the original
children's version
of
*Fifty Shades of Grey*.

948.

Consent doesn't speak in code.

Getting naked is not code for consent.
Sending a nude is not code for consent.
Saying 'I love you' is not code for consent.
Going on a date is not code for consent.
Drinking or dancing is not code for consent.
Even consent to one certain sex act
is not code for consent to all kinds of sex acts, or sex of the same act
again, or sex with somebody else.

The only code for consent
is consent itself.

949.

Consent to take a nude
is not consent for sharing it.


The difference between
a *sent* nude and a *leaked* nude
is consent.


More accurately,
the difference between
a *sent* nude and a *leaked* nude
is the difference between
*consent* and *slut-shaming*.


Sending nudes is not a violation.
Leaking nudes is a violation-
the purpose of that violation
is to slut-shame women for what they sexually consented to do.


Our consent in sending a nude,
is not an open invitation for leaking that nude.
And we shouldn't be slut-shamed for what we consent to do.


Let's normalize shaming the perpetrator
for leaking the nude
instead of slut-shaming the victim
for sending the nude,
because in doing so
we reinforce a consent culture
without sexual shaming.

Let's normalize
women consenting
to sending
their own nudes.
Let's shame
men for sharing them
with other dudes.

Let's normalize
women consenting
to expressing their sexuality.
Let's shame
men who think that a woman's sexuality
is theirs to share.

950.

Men proudly send dick pics
to strangers
without even being asked.

And no shame smudges their name,
even if that picture got broadcast-
because 'boys will be boys'
and they're just having a blast.

But women are shamed
for sending nudes-
to a boyfriend who begged for it
and then betrayed her
by leaking it to his dudes.

A man's reputation is always intact
but a woman's is slandered.

I'm going to change that
by taking a nude of myself,
while fucking your double standards.

951.

Consent to nakedness
is not consent to sex.

Consent to nakedness
can be for a variety of reasons;
I feel hot, I'm more comfortable naked, I like a certain style of
revealing clothing, I'm posing for a nude, I'm going into the shower,
etc.

A man assuming that
my consent to nakedness
is consent to sex,
is as ridiculous as
if my gynaecologist assumes
my consent to nakedness
is consent to sex.

952.

At my gynaecologist appointment
I lift up my dress
I take off my underwear
I spread my legs,
I consent to my vagina being prodded
and despite all of the above I'm STILL
not consenting to sex.
So outside my gynaecologist appointment
what the fuck makes you think
that my mini dress
or my nakedness
or my drunkenness
or my whatever else
besides an eager YES
is consent to sex?

Fuckboy, lest you'd like
to be indicted-
you don't come to this party
only if and unless and until and when
you're fucking invited.

953.

Do I have to give you
a trigger warning
before I tell you about the rape
that happened to me
without any
warning?

It wasn't morning
and I wasn't wearing
a short dress-
but it was a textbook rape
where you say "no"
and they hear it as "yes".

There was no consent
and no contest-
he won.

For a moment,
then he was gone.

The prize was my body for a moment
and as a loser I spent,
years with the trauma
until it became my best friend.

No one tells you this.
There is no therapist
that will save you
no help-me book
that will get you closer

to closure.

Only you can step out of the darkness.

Each step takes you closer.

At first, to that night, to the fight, you have to push through it again
until you see the light.

Your body is born anew every day.
You have a choice not to give it away
to the trauma
that fucks your head each night.

Take a step. I promise. No warning.
You will be alright.

I know
because...

I think
I'm alright.

954.

Reminder:
You are not
what you did not
consent to.


Let's normalize
the notion that
what happens
to a victim
does not define
the victim.
Instead,
it defines
the perpetrator.

955.

Ask yourself; why do men resort to rape women when there are plenty of legal and consensual ways that men can have sex with women? The issue is not that men do not have access to sex; the issue is that they want access to rape. Because rape is not sex. The issue is not that men do not understand consent; the issue is that they don't want to. Because consent threatens their control.

\*\*\*

I do not buy the idea that men do not understand consent when having sex with women. They are very vocal if a woman does something to them that they don't like (say for example if a woman accidently uses her teeth in a blow job). This means that not only do they know the basic concept of consent, but also that they actively ignore it when the boundary isn't violating their own bodies.

956.

Why are you dressed like that?
Don't blame men if they rape!
*But remember*...not all men rape.
But you still shouldn't dress like that.
Otherwise it's your fault
men can't control themselves.
*But remember*...not all men lack self-control.
But you still shouldn't blindly trust men-
don't go out late or alone or with that guy you met online.
*But remember*...not all men are dangerous, at least not all the time.
But don't step out of line,
just in case
you need to be safe
carry a pepper spray can
clutch your keys like a weapon.
*But remember...not all men...*
*...not all men...not all men...*


\*\*\*


To justify rape by saying
"men can't control themselves"
you are insulting ALL MEN
who can control themselves

957.

**Society:** *Not all men* are dangerous, but women shouldn't be out late because they risk getting attacked by men!

**Women:** Why don't men stay at home when it's late, since they present the threat?

**Society:** That's ridiculous! We can't lock up ALL MEN - we don't know which of them are likely to attack.

**Women:** So not all men attack, but ALL WOMEN have a chance to be attacked?

**Society:** Yes.

**Women:** So as a woman if I'm out late, how can I know which men will attack and which men won't?

**Society:** Just be wary of all men.

**Women:** So it is ALL MEN then?

**Society:** ...

958.

Men scream
NOT ALL MEN
at strange women,
and in the same breath
tell their mothers, sisters
girlfriends, wives, and daughters
to be wary of ALL MEN.

Men want to ensure that strange women
trust all men
so that they can exploit their availability to them,
and in the same breath
they don't want the women they already own
to be exploited by other men.

959.

I have a superpower.

I can eradicate
the male gaze,
I can avert their eyes
from rolling all over
my body.

I have a superpower.

I can become
*The Invisible Woman-*
the one that no man
can see.

But to achieve that superpower
my husband has to be walking
right next to me.


*** 


Men only respect you
when you're owned by
another man-
otherwise they think you're fair game
for them to claim.

960.

The men
who interrupt women expressing valid fears of men
to say "not all men"
are the reason why
it is "all men".

Because when they cannot even let me
express my valid fears *verbally*
without interrupting me, angrily,
imagine what they'll do to me *physically*
when I express my lack of consent.

\*\*\*

What goes on
in the mind of a man
who sees my limbs
as a feast,
yet rages when I
call him 'a beast'?

Perhaps you need to look more
into my eyes
instead of at my thighs
to see,
why
I fear
the way
you look at me.

961.

"NOT ALL MEN ARE RAPISTS"
they scream.

As if that will make the problem of rape seem
unrelated to gender.

Not all men are rapists
but the fact is
99% of rapists
are men,
this is based on reports
by the Bureau of Justice Statistics.
Wish-washing that fact doesn't help anyone
except protect the men
who are rapists.


NOT ALL MEN
ARE RAPISTS!

But all rapists
are men.


N.B. 99% of rapists are men. (Source: Bureau of Justice Statistics
report on Sex Offenses and Offenders).

962.

I'd rather treat **all men**
as potential predators
even if they get *offended*,
than assume **not all men**
are potential predators
and end up getting *assaulted.*

NOT ALL MEN ARE RAPISTS
but we don't know which ones aren't.
And I'd rather hurt your feelings
than have my body violated.

Treating **all men**
as potential predators
may *hurt their feelings*,
but assuming **not all men**
are potential predators
may *cause my assault.*

N.B. According to the Bureau of Justice Statistics report on Sex
Offenses and Offenders; 99% of rapists are men, and 91% of rape
victims are women. And unfortunately, rapists don't walk around with
a warning alert. So if you truly care about women (and you aren't a
rapist), our rational fears won't offend you- but instead, you will be
offended by the behaviour of other men.

963.

A man follows a woman to give her his phone number.
In his mind his harmless action is no cause to ponder.

But the woman he's following
doesn't know what he intends to be doing,
she just knows from past experience
what men who follow her do.

They may be harmless, that's true,
but equally they may catcall, stalk, rape, or attack.

When you follow a woman
(no matter how harmless your intention is)
make sure you understand that.

We are afraid of you.

Our fear protects us more than
concerns of offending you.

And here's something else for you to ponder;
perhaps we don't want your fucking phone number.

\*\*\*

NOT ALL MEN
hate
attack
abuse

rape.
BUT ALL WOMEN
live with the fear of getting
hated
attacked
abused
raped.

964.

Dear All Men,
No
we don't know
which one of you
is the good guy and which is bad.
You don't walk around with labels,
and we won't walk around with chances.
Sincerely,
All Women.

965.

Dear Men,
I have my guards up around you.
All my guards up, around all of you,
and if you're confused as to why
search for #MeToo.
It happened to me,
to my mother, to my sister,
to my best friend-
I cannot pretend
that I'm not afraid,
in order not to offend
your gender
while my gender
has been betrayed
by yours.
Like the ocean
when out of the blue
it rapes the shores.
Like Gretel's
pebbles
I have built
the safest trail
to get back home,
at the safest time.
(Exactly a couple of minutes
before nine).
I've pretended to be on the phone
so that men would leave me alone.
I've crossed red pedestrian lights
to escape catcallers,
because I'd rather be hit by a car

than be hit on by stalkers.
I've avoided looking men in the eye-
because the way they look at my body
revolts me to the point where I'd rather
no longer see
how they objectify.
And no, it doesn't matter what I wear
because they'll still strip me
with their glare.
I send the details of my new date
to my best friend-
in case I go missing,
she'll know where to send
help.
I've heard my neighbour yelp,
from the bruises her husband
leaves on her body each night-
so it's not just from strange men
but especially from the closest ones
I feel the fright.
Will my husband too
suddenly turn into
a dragon,
after being my knight?
Did you know?
The United Nations Women
national studies show,
that up to 70% of women
have experienced violence
from a man they already know.
And according to the
Bureau of Justice statistics
on sex offenders and offenses,

99% of rapists are men
91% of rape victims are women.
Statistically,
it is safer for me
to protect myself from *all men*
(until they prove otherwise),
than assume that *not all men*
can be wolves in disguise.
The story of the *Little Red Riding Hood*
speaks the reality of our lives.
If this truth offends you-
reflect
on why you expect
women to massage your ego
with lies.


Dear Men,
I have my guards up around you.
All my guards up, around all of you,
because I have to be prepared.
I say this not because I hate you-
I say it because I love you
but I want to love you
without being afraid.

966.

"WHAT ABOUT MALE VICTIMS OF RAPE?"
he asks to interrupt
when I'm talking about
female victims of rape.

"What about them?" I reply
"99% of rapists are men
so both males AND females are more likely to be raped by men-
we're talking about
the exact same
problem".

967.

Consent is a two-way street
and it knows no gender.

Assuming that men are
'always ready', 'sex crazy', 'never say no',
is part of patriarchal culture,
that celebrates men as rapists
but never raped by another.

But men do get raped
by women, and by each other.
And this is how they suffer;
they pay with their silence
to uphold the patriarchy
for one another.

968.

The kind of person
who thinks rape can be joked about,
is the kind of person
who thinks rape isn't a serious offence.


\*\*\*


Saying:
"She's too ugly to get raped"

is as ridiculous as saying:

"He's too handsome to be a rapist"


\*\*\*


"You're too ugly to get raped..."
also means
"rape is a compliment
reserved for beautiful women".

"At least he doesn't hit you..."
also means
"we have set the bar that low for you".


N.B. Italy's top court has opened a probe into a sentence by an

Ancona appeals court that found the victim in a rape case was "too ugly to be raped". (Source: www.euronews.com).

969.

"Only pretty girls get raped"
he tells me
as he rapes me.

As if rape is the ultimate
compliment (or punishment?)
for being pretty.

I was too young to see
the trauma that this would
turn out to be.

I believed him. I was pretty.
So I was happy.

I believed him.
And not only
did I believe
that I deserved
to be raped,
but the bigger disaster;
is that I also
longed for the rape
for long after...

970.

I'm a woman
who has never ever
received an unsolicited
dick pic.

And here's the fucked up thing;
I often wonder
whether not getting one
is a good
or a bad thing?

Because we are conditioned to see
the entitlement of fuckboys towards women
as a validation of our desirability as women.

971.

Sis,
that catcall isn't a compliment;
he didn't throw
that sexual comment,
to flatter.
The patriarchy has conditioned you
to view
his dangerous exercise of domination
as a validation,
for your sexiness to matter.


\*\*\*


The women who claim that catcalling is a compliment
have been catcalled in contexts
where their race or status
or whatever other privilege they have over the catcaller
played a major role in the incident
to not leave the woman feeling threatened,
so she mistook the catcalling as a compliment.

972.

To the man who doesn't understand
the difference between
'complimenting' and 'catcalling'-
here's a simple way
to distinguish one from the other;
before speaking
ask yourself,
"Would I say this to my mother?"

973.

I don't need strange men to tell me
that I'm pretty
because I have a mirror
and I already know that I am.

Their egos assume women need their opinions
and that we must give a damn.

974.

"How old were you when you were first harassed?"
my girl friend asked.

I don't remember.

I don't remember because I've always seen it as a normal price to pay
for being a girl who has turned into a woman.
I saw it happen to other girls and women
and I never thought it was odd.

It was a rite of passage actually
an indication you've gone from child to woman;
a precedent.

It took me 3 decades to realize
harassment shouldn't be
a normal event.

975.

I was 14.

I wore a fitted dress.
My boyfriend told me that his father
said I was asking for sex.

I wasn't asking for sex.

I was taken aback by the remark
coming from a man the age of my father
whom I thought saw me as a daughter.

It took years to grasp the concept;
our bodies, as girls and women,
are property of the male gaze
they tell us what our bodies
are trying to say
in each context and place,
and we're supposed to just nod
and agree.
Because this is a man's world
and women exist in it as the image
that men want us to be.

976.

Girls don't mature faster than boys.

Girls are treated like women,
while boys are treated as boys.

Girls are seen as too young to vote
but not too young to get married.

Girls are seen as too young for an abortion
but not too young to be mothers.

Girls are seen as too young to make a major decision;
but never too young to be held with
the accountability of a woman.

977.

"She wore a short skirt- what did she expect?"

"She was out late- what did she expect?"

"She was drunk- what did she expect?"

"He's a single guy - what did she expect?"

"He's a sexual creature- what did she expect?"

"He can't help it- what did she expect?"

Victim blaming women
is when they are blamed
for what they have done
AND for what men have done to them.


Victim blaming women
has no logic other than
to twist the narrative
to make women always wrong
and men always right.
It started from Adam and Eve
when he blamed her
because he ate the apple that night.


But remember that when you blame female victims
for the way they dress
for the way their "no" could be mistaken for a "yes"
for anything else,

when you blame female victims
you are also saying ALL MEN
are beasts, nonetheless.

978.

I know this is not a woman's world when I hear people say:
"She was wearing shorts,
she shouldn't expose her body like that"


I know this is a man's world when I don't hear people say;
"He was wearing shorts,
he shouldn't expose his body like that"



\*\*\*



Women *are* oppressed
because they *are*
attacked by men.

Men *feel* oppressed
when they are told
*not to attack* women.

979.

"Was it my fault?"
asked my bright pink dress.

"Was it my fault?"
asked my lipstick stain mess.

"Was it my fault?"
asked my tanned slender legs.

"Was it my fault?"
asked my female sex.

"Was it my fault?"
asked my tongue that never said 'yes'.

"Was it my fault?"
asked the dark alleyway to my home address.

"Was it my fault?"
asked the full moon in her distress.


"Yes- it is my fault"
answers the rapist,
who will never confess.

980.

Do you blame the rocks
for being too hard?
Do you blame the sands
for being too soft?

Do you blame the oceans
for their fast moving tide?
Do you blame the skies
for their slow moving clouds?

Do you blame the sun
for being too hot?
Do you blame the moon
for going out too late?

So then why
do you blame yourself?

981.

YOU attacked me.

Then you blamed it
on what I said
on what I did
on what I wore.

YOU attacked me.
And I won't take
YOUR blame for it
anymore.

***

If you are justifying
why women
get raped by men-
you are defending
men for raping
women.

And if you are defending
men for raping
women-
you are defending
rape.

982.

Me too.

Can you believe me, too?

Can you believe me even when
I can't put the horror into words
because they won't sit
in the script,
as obediently as I did?
I said 'no' politely
I didn't know how to force him to stop
the way he forced me to keep going.
A minute of his life, in mine it's ongoing.
Can you believe me even when
I tell you of a familiar pain
of a non-fiction
that just makes me the same
as so many women
you claim
are just statistics you don't know.
Perhaps liars
turned actors
putting on an attention shit-show.
Can you tell me, as a director,
in the next scene, where do we go?
Or perhaps how many times
and how loud
should we say *no*?

983.

They say what if she is lying?

What if she is framing,
that boy with the rape?

Yet when the boy cried wolf
lying again and again.
He was eventually *believed* to be a liar.

None of the sheep
planned an escape.

***

We'd rather believe men even when
we have reason to know they are lying,
over believing women even when
we have no reason to know they are lying.

984.

Men fear false rape claims
and
women fear actual rape.

And while false rape claims
rarely happen,
actual rape
has never been
out of fashion.

***

The reason
you think
women lie
about getting raped,
is because
men lie
about not raping.

985.

"So you choose to believe women
without any evidence?"
he asks, in a fit
"this #MeToo movement is bullshit!"

"So you choose to discredit women
without any evidence, too?"
I ask,
"I believe women
because I believe that you do-
know what it takes, the stakes
of speaking out in a world
full of assholes like you!"

986.

If men spoke out
about
actual rape,
with the same conviction
they do for false rape claims,
we would eliminate rape
and false rape claims.

987.

Do you know why
the man falsely accused of rape
cannot get rid of the social stigma
even when
he is proven
innocent?

Because we know
that there are so many actual rapists
that get away with rape
despite crippling incriminating evidence.

So how can we know
that the man falsely accused
is truly innocent,
and not another rapist
lucky enough to lack evidence?

Social stigmas are based on a precedent.

To remove the social stigma
that makes the falsely accused suffer-
we need to hold rapists accountable
instead of holding them with a buffer.

988.

We should ask
"What was the man thinking?"
instead of
"What was the woman wearing?"


And instead of asking her;
"Did you say NO?"
we should ask him;
"Did she say YES?"


*** 


Don't fucking ask her
"Did you say NO? Did you fight him off?",
because in doing so
you are perpetuating that
the *mere existence*
of her body
is an open invitation
for men
to help themselves!


It's always a NO- until, and if, and only, and when, she says YES!

989.

You question why I didn't speak up;
tell him to stop
report him immediately,
why did I endure
so silently?

You blame me.

You blame me.

My tongue is tied-
the mute is on
repeat.
Silence,
is my strategy
of defeat.

But why?
Because I wanted to live
even when the pain made me die.

When you're a child
and the ones responsible for your survival
are also the ones who are violent-
you quickly learn that to survive
you must stay silent.

And then suddenly
you become an adult.
And if you don't speak up
everyone assume it's your fault.

But how can you expect me
to know how to speak up?!
My tongue is numb
from the many times
I was told to shut up!

It will take time for me to learn
how to unlearn what was normalized-
I'm an adult teaching myself
what I was never taught as a child.

990.

I am one of the 75%
who never once
reported
that I was raped
twice.

Both times, with people I know.
Both times, I clearly said NO.
Both times, they heard me
but did not stop or even slow.
Both times, there were no other
witnesses to their crime show.

And I know.

That if I report them with the evidence I lack, it will not be enough-
I will lose both cases, and I will lose both people
that I complicatedly
still love.

N.B. 3 out of 4 sexual assaults are never reported to the police.
(Source: RAINN- Rape, Abuse & Incest National Network).

991.

Women are groomed
to master silence.

Even silence
isn't as silent
as our silence.

They tell us it's taboo to talk about our sex lives,
so that we have no notes to compare
on the abuse we endure from men
and the lies
so that we do not realize
we got raped.

We silence our bodies
under layers of drape,
and we silence our voices
until our lips become jails
that we cannot escape.

***

When we talk about our sexual assault
it shifts the narrative
from the shame we feel
to the shaming of the abuser.

When we are finally ready
to talk about our sexual assault;

it means we finally understand
it was never our fault.

992.

You teach me, as a woman,
that my most valued asset
is my body,
but when I get raped
you tell me to hush
and not make a big deal...
stop playing victim
it's not the worst ordeal.

Yet when I have sex
with my body
with whomever I want
consensually,
you slut shame me
and even subject me
to an honour killing.

So my body, is my most valued asset,
only when it is being *abused by you*?

Are you fucking kidding?

993.

How fucked up is it
that driving while drunk
is a crime,
but raping while drunk
is an excuse?!


\*\*\*


Drunk driving
is punishable by law,
but being drunk
is a legal defence for rape.
This policy attempts to shape
the idea that it is not okay
for a man to ride his car
while drunk,
but it is excusable
for a man to ride a woman
while drunk.

Think about it.
Think about a society
that gives more rights to cars
than it gives to women's bodies.


N.B. In South Korea, being drunk is a legal defence for rape. (Source:

"Sim Sin Mi Yak" and "Joo Chi Gam Hyung").

994.

When, to be safe,
women are expected to pay
for a pepper spray
can
and self-defence classes;
capitalism and patriarchy
are telling the masses
that only women who can afford to be safe
deserve to be safe
and the absurdity of that is tacit.

995.

The raping of women is a profitable industry.

Think about it, for a second, with me.

The raping of women creates demand for:
-Rape test kits
-Investigators
-Police
-Lawyers
-Judges
-Courtrooms
-Perhaps abortions
-STD medications
-Therapists

And leaving rape cases lingering and unresolved
makes men more confident and bold
about getting away with rape,
hence women fear that no matter what
they have no escape.
This creates more
demand for:
-Self-defence classes
-Pepper spray cans
-Rape whistles
-And whatever other illusion to make us feel safe.

What a life we pave!

The raping of women also upholds the patriarchy;
the fear of getting raped

in itself rapes
the mind of a woman
and controls her sexual behaviour:
-She won't go out late
-Won't go out with any date
-Worries about what to wear
-Covers her thighs and her hair
because otherwise, she's taught,
that rape is her fault.

The raping of women profits the economy
and the patriarchy,
thus it is not in their benefit
to treat it as a serious crime.

Perhaps that is why
rape remains an issue
in our modern day and time.

N.B. Only a third of reported rape cases are cleared. (Source: FBI's Uniform Crime Reporting 2017 crime in the United States, ucr.fbi.gov).

996.

No I don't want a gun.
I don't want a pepper spray can.
I don't want to clutch my keys between my fingers.
I don't want to be on alert from any man.

I want to be safe.


I do not want to
protect myself from men.

I want a world wherein
men are not dangerous.

997.

Safe spaces for girls and women?

I was followed by a man
so I took the first exit
into a *woman's only* toilet
because it's a safe space for women
right?

Wrong.
He followed me in.
Placed his palm under my chin.
Told me he just wanted
a taste of heaven.
I must be the devil
for not giving it to him.


Safe spaces for girls and women?

The boys in high school would peep
inside the *girls only* changing rooms
before P.E. class
through a hole
in the key lock on the door.
Then they'd call us sluts
because they saw us in our underwear.
Never mind we didn't even know
they were there.


Safe spaces for girls and women?

At the *girls only* high school
college boys are packed in the parking lot
afterschool
looking at us like meat to pick,
flashing us a real life version
of their dick pic.


Safe spaces for girls and women?

There's a pink taxi in Dubai
*driven*
*by women*
*and only takes female clientele.*
When I was attacked in a regular taxi
I was told "oh well,
your fault for not getting a pink taxi!"


Do you fucking see?
The shame, the victim blame,
the entitlement and audacity,
in the safe spaces for girls and women?!


Safe spaces for girls and women
are never actually safe
if they are in a world
that isn't safe
for girls and women.

998.

Gender segregated spaces
in cultures that encourage abstaining
from sexual attraction,
are just another way of detraction,
of delegitimizing and of disregarding
non-heterosexual sexual attraction.

***

Gender segregated
toilets, buses,
schools, gyms, etc.
Remind me of
racial segregation.

Until everyone is given access to the same spaces
safely and without gender discrimination,
how can we expect equality and safety
for the current
and future generation?

999.

I don't want safe spaces for women.

I don't want segregated
schools, locker rooms,
gyms, activities,
toilets, malls,
or public transportation.
The only thing this does
is normalize the notion
that women are only safe
in isolation.
I want women to be safe
in every space
in every location.
This is a woman's world
as much as it's a man's world;
our safety
must be
a public declaration.

1000.

Women, all women, deserve to be safe while
*walking home alone
*wearing shorts
*dancing at a club
*drinking
*being alone with a man/ men.


All women deserve to be safe while
*they do,
*anything that all men
*are safe to do, too.

*To the one still holding this book:*
*There's still more…*


*So much more shit!*

Made in the USA
Columbia, SC
15 September 2024

41840925R00186